MARK TWAIN

and his World

MARK TWAIN

and his World

Justin Kaplan

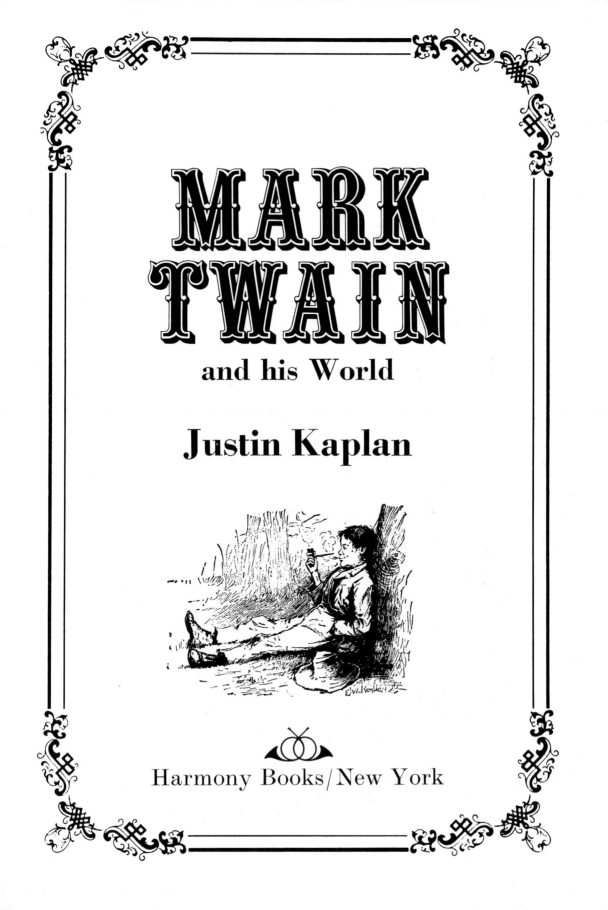

Harmony Books/New York

This edition published in 1982 by Harmony Books, a division of Crown
Publishers, Inc., One Park Avenue, New York, New York 10016 and
simultaneously in Canada by General Publishing Company Limited.
First published by Simon and Schuster Inc. 1974

HARMONY BOOKS and ◢⟨Ⓧ⟩◣ are trademarks of Crown Publishers, Inc.

This book was designed and produced by
George Rainbird Ltd, 40 Park Street, London W1Y 4DE

This edition printed and bound by
Toppan Printing Co. (S) PTE. Ltd. Singapore
Color origination by Westerham Press,
Westerham, England

Library of Congress Cataloging in Publication Data
Kaplan, Justin.
Mark Twain and his world.

Reprint. Originally published: New York : Joseph,
1974.
Includes index.
1. Twain, Mark, 1835–1910. 2. Authors, American—
19th century—Biography. I. Title.
[PS1331.K325 1983]   818'.409 [B]   82–9201
AACR2

ISBN: 0–517–548836
10 9 8 7 6 5 4 3 2 1

First Harmony Edition

For Susanna, Hester and Polly

Contents

Color Plates

Acknowledgments

Material from Mark Twain Papers copyright 1966 by The Mark Twain Company.

Excerpts from *Mark Twain's Autobiography*, Volumes I and II, edited by Albert Bigelow Paine. Copyright, 1924, by Clara Gabrilowitsch; renewed 1952 by Clara Clemens Samossoud. By permission of Harper & Row, Publishers, Inc.

Excerpts from *The Love Letters of Mark Twain*, edited by Dixon Wecter. Copyright, 1947, 1949 by The Mark Twain Company. By permission of Harper & Row, Publishers, Inc.

Excerpts from *Mark Twain in Eruption*, edited by Bernard DeVoto. Copyright, 1922 by Harper & Row, Publishers, Inc. Copyright, 1940 by The Mark Twain Company. By permission of Harper & Row, Publishers, Inc.

Excerpts from *Mark Twain's Notebook*, edited by Albert Bigelow Paine. Copyright, 1935 by The Mark Twain Company. By permission of Harper & Row, Publishers, Inc.

Paine's letter to Harper, 1926 in *Mark Twain: God's Fool* by Hamlin Hill. Copyright © 1973 by The Mark Twain Company. By permission of Harper & Row, Publishers, Inc.

Excerpts from *Mark Twain—Howells Letters*, edited by Henry Nash Smith and William M. Gibson. Published by The Belknap Press of Harvard University Press, 1960. By permission of Harvard University Press and The Mark Twain Company.

Excerpts from *Mark Twain's Hannibal, Huck & Tom*, edited by Walter Blair. Originally published by the University of California Press; reprinted by permission of The Regents of the University of California.

Excerpts from *Mark Twain's Correspondence with Henry Huttleston Rogers, 1893–1909*, edited by Lewis Leary. Originally published by the University of California Press; reprinted by permission of The Regents of the University of California.

Chapter One

Hannibal and the River
1835–61

Two currents flowed through Mark Twain's life. One flowed outward and away from the river town of Hannibal, Missouri, toward the nation and the world; the other flowed back home again. Hannibal was the scene of his boyhood, but it remained one of the principal dwelling places of his imagination. Out of the opposition of these currents came a legendary life and a dazzling presence, one of the shaping styles of America's literature and thought, half a dozen of its major books, and such a range of enterprise and concern that in the end Mark Twain is more imposing than the sum of his work. He eludes definitions and categories. He was 'sole, incomparable', his friend William Dean Howells said, unlike all the other 'literary men' Howells had known. Mark Twain brought to the occupation of humorist a greater profundity, power, and artistry than it had ever had in his country. But 'humorist' is not enough to describe him, especially since his own experience demonstrated that in America 'humorist' tended to imply the adjective 'mere', and the synonym 'buffoon'. 'Author' is too bland; 'man of letters' suggests precisely what his vernacular impulses rejected; 'novelist' describes only a part of his achievement. Social and political criticism runs through his entire career, from *The Gilded Age* on, but such criticism was the distinctive concern of his old age, when he was also occupied with that anomalous and sprawling masterpiece, his autobiography. In his life he had seen so much and comprehended so much that when he died in 1910 America said goodbye to one of its authentic sages and seers and also to its own young manhood as a nation.

Opposite *'I came in with Halley's comet in 1835.'*

In a sense Mark Twain spent his career writing, from a lengthening distance in time and space, about Hannibal, about what began to seem the most memorable boyhood ever lived, and about the contrasts of his real or imagined Hannibal with the world as he knew it. *Tom Sawyer* and *Huckleberry Finn* are the most celebrated of his many attempts to recreate the town—there are letters, rough sketches, notebooks, autobiographical material, the flow of his mind and talk. Often he wrote about Hannibal as 'St Petersburg'—literally, 'heaven'. But in time his vision of 'the white town drowsing in the sunshine of a summer's morning' grew more supple and complex, until it embraced hell as well as heaven, the present as well as the past, the darkest as well as the brightest possibilities of the human condition. Resolving the opposed currents of his life, Hannibal itself became an image of the great world beyond it, at the same time the most general and the most particularized of Mark Twain's fictions. But Hannibal also had a location in historical time and space and in the great tide of America's westward expansion that swept Mark Twain's family along with it.

His father and mother, as he once acknowledged, had an almost miraculous faculty for finding the eddies and backwaters of this tide. A vigorous young country was discovering its riches, but the Clemenses followed a pattern of decline. Their pendulum swung in a narrowing arc between expectation and disappointment, then between want and bankruptcy, and in the course of their forced moves to smaller and shabbier quarters they shed the piano, the family spoons, and the tea service. By the end of 1846, when Mark Twain was eleven years old, there was no longer much furniture left for the sheriff to seize, and the family—which also included a daughter, Pamela, nineteen, and the favorite, Henry, seven—boarded above a drugstore in Hannibal. Orion, the eldest son, was in St Louis working as a printer, a step down in the world for the son of his parents.

In 1823 John Marshall Clemens, lawyer and storekeeper, settled with his bride, Jane Lampton, in Columbia, Kentucky. They had a common background: their families had been slaveholders and small landowners in the South, poor gentry, but gentry nevertheless; and, as Mark Twain was to recall with some amusement, his parents were Virginians and ancestor-proud. Marshall Clemens (named, in a hopeful mood, after the Virginian who was to become Chief Justice of the Supreme Court) was descended from one of the regicide judges who sent King Charles I of England to the headsman's block, while the Lamptons grandly traced their connection to the earls of Durham and even considered taking steps to claim the title when it fell vacant. Although he was to ridicule

*In 1847 the Clemenses lived here with another family above what was then a
drugstore*

the whole title business, Mark Twain entertained himself from time to
time with a fantasy that he had become Earl of Durham, wrote a novel
called *The American Claimant*, and had a lifelong passion for claimants
of all sorts, including the Tichborne Claimant Arthur Orton, Satan, the
Veiled Prophet of Khorassan, Louis XVII, Mary Baker Eddy, and, in his
view, that false claimant William Shakespeare.

Jane Clemens in her eighties said that she had married 'in a pet', to
spite another man, and whether this was truth or imagining, it still
suggests that although they were well matched in background Mark

Twain's father and mother were at best not wholly compatible through-out their twenty-four years together. In character and personality they were antithetic. Play, humor, laughter, tenderness—Mark Twain saw these chiefly in his mother. 'She was of a sunshiny disposition, and her long life was mainly a holiday to her,' he wrote. 'She always had the heart of a young girl.' Through all the family troubles she maintained a kind of perky stoicism, which was lightened considerably by her love for gossip, gaudy spectacles like parades and funerals, bright colors, and animals.

But Mark Twain described his father as 'stern, unsmiling, never demonstrated affection for wife or child. . . . Silent, austere, of perfect probity and high principle; ungentle of manner toward his children, but always a gentleman in his phrasing—and never punished them—a look was enough, and more than enough. . . . It was remembered that he went to church—once; never again.'

Like his father the son was to be an agnostic and an anticleric, and not the least of the many changes Mark Twain would see in his lifetime was the decline of the Protestant clergy in influence and leadership; the pulpit, he was to say, had become about as indispensable as 'the sun—the moon, anyway'. It was the 'sunshiny' mother, at the same time an enthusiastic and 'abandoned' Presbyterian, who subjected young

Birthplace, Florida, Missouri. 'Heretofore I have always stated it was a palace, but I shall be more guarded now.' Autobiography

Clemens to a religion of chronic anxiety and certain damnation which, although he later rejected it, reinforced his lifelong sense of wrongdoing, his obsession with conscience, and his inability to disabuse himself altogether of a belief in the reality of hell and Satan. He was to look back with 'shuddering horror upon the days when I believed I believed'.

Dreaming of great riches and also haunted by a fear of sinking in the world, Marshall Clemens invested his hopes and his assets in what turned out to be a series of disasters. He left Kentucky and moved to Fentress County, Tennessee, where he eventually acquired about seventy thousand acres of virgin land. He expected to become rich on the coal, copper, and iron ore that supposedly lay in the soil where potatoes and wild grass were growing. In this expectation, which never panned out in his or his children's lifetime, he laid upon the shoulders of the Clemens family what Mark Twain called the heavy curse of prospective wealth: 'It is good to begin life poor; it is good to begin life rich— these are wholesome; but to begin it poor and *prospectively* rich! The man who has not experienced it cannot imagine the curse of it.'

Meanwhile, in search of more immediate rewards, Marshall Clemens followed the tide of settlement across the Mississippi into Missouri, where he became a storekeeper in the crossroads hamlet of Florida. It was there, on 30 November 1835, that Jane Clemens gave birth to the sixth of their seven children, Samuel, named after his paternal grand-father. Halley's comet blazed in the night sky when he was born, just as it would when he died in April 1910. By then, 'light years' removed from Florida, he had come to think of himself and the comet as 'unaccountable freaks' who, since they had come in together, 'must go out together'.

Marshall Clemens became a county judge in Florida but failed to make a go of it as storekeeper, and in 1839 he moved his family for the last time, forty miles east to the Mississippi, to Hannibal. There, in addition to seeking a living from several mercantile ventures, none of which thrived, he served as justice of the peace, practicing attorney, president of the Library Association, and chairman of the Committee on Roads. He was accounted one of the first citizens of the town. Even so, until he died in 1847 at the age of forty-nine, Judge Clemens continued to follow his fading star into poverty, dispossession, bankruptcy, exhaustion, and hopelessness. He had failed in the law, in business, in land speculation, and even in a venture or two in slave trading. On his deathbed he kissed his daughter Pamela; as Mark Twain remembered into his old age, this was the only display of affection that anyone in the family had ever seen. 'He did not say goodbye to his wife or to any but his daughter,' the son wrote fifty years later; and he added the cryptic note, 'The Autopsy'. He was referring to something he had never been able to forget: secretly, and in horror, the twelve-year-old boy had witnessed a post-mortem examination of his father. 'My father died this day 63 years ago,' he wrote to his daughter Clara on 24 March 1910. 'I remember all about it quite clearly.'

These were some of the family backgrounds of Mark Twain, who all his life hungered for affection. He was capable of great rage and greater remorse, and was sometimes like a child demanding attention and approval in a nursery as big as the world. He could never separate the idyl of boyhood from the terror. And as a miner in the West, and later as businessman, speculator, and publisher caught up in the scramble of the Gilded Age, he repeated his father's pattern—he lived in dread of debt but within sight of enormous prospective wealth, and he went broke.

It was a near thing that Sam survived his first years at all. Three of Jane's children died before the age of ten, and he had been a sickly infant who was born two months prematurely and hung precariously onto life. For his first seven years, as he joked, he lived mainly on cod-liver oil and on the allopathic medicines his mother favored in the hope of driving out one disease by inducing the symptoms of another. Jane's medicines worked, or at least they failed to kill him. He grew into manhood sparely built, small-boned, with narrow sloping shoulders, delicate hands, and tapering fingers, all in contrast to his thick eyebrows and a great unruly shock of hair—sandy through adolescence and then darkening to auburn —which he tried to tame by soaking it and then plastering it down.*

His head, like a child's, seemed too large for his body, not large enough for his strangely narrowed, glimmering gray-green eyes ('so eaglelike,' Bret Harte said, 'that a second lid would not have surprised me'). He had a slow, drawling habit of speech, something that he acquired from his mother and learned to make the most of when he told stories, but he regarded it as an infirmity, like a stammer, and he was sensitive about it, just as he was fastidious. Although he described himself as being 'as sociable as a fly', unlike Western Americans of his time he detested pawing or even touching other people, and in his old age, especially when he took to wearing white suits, he made a fetish of cleanliness. He

---

* 'When red-headed people are above a certain social grade,' his Connecticut Yankee was to say, 'their hair is auburn.'

Opposite *Raftsmen Playing Cards by George Caleb Bingham, 1847. (Detail.) 'The annual processions of mighty rafts that used to glide by Hannibal when I was a boy.'* Life on the Mississippi

was troubled with nightmares when he was young, and often he walked in his sleep. Years later he explored this nocturnal way of life, the dark side of his moon, and he concluded, 'From the cradle up I have been like the rest of the race—never quite sane in the night.'

Sam Clemens turned four a week or so after he was brought to Hannibal in November 1839. It was to be his home for thirteen and a half years, at the end of which he set out on his travels and never returned except in memory and for brief scattered visits. When he came back for the last time, in 1902, he said that everything in the town must have shrunk. He posed for photographers in the doorway of the family's two-story frame house on Hill Street. 'It all seems so small to me,' he said. 'I suppose if I should come back here ten years from now it would be the size of a birdhouse.'

Yet, for the boy born in the crossroads settlement of Florida, Hannibal was nothing less than a world of its own, bounded north, south, and west by an Eden wilderness and, as he looked eastward toward the dense forests on the Illinois shore, by 'the great Mississippi, the majestic, the magnificent Mississippi, rolling its mile-wide tide along, shining in the sun'. The river offered adventure, travel, and what seemed the most gorgeous of all occupations. 'When I was a boy, there was but one permanent ambition among my comrades,' he was to write in *Life on the Mississippi*, 'That was, to be a steamboatman.' It outlasted the ambition to become a pirate or join the circus. Outside the town were other natural wonders: Holliday's Hill, towering steeply above the river; Glasscock's Island, a place for camping and hiding; Bear Creek, where boys swam and fished in the summer, skated in winter; and, among the bluffs two miles south of town, Dr McDowell's limestone cave, its entrance guarded with an iron door.

When he was only sixteen years old Sam Clemens, under the signature 'S. L. C.', made his first appearances in Eastern periodicals as Hannibal's chronicler. 'The Dandy Frightening the Squatter', a frontier sketch published in *The Carpet-Bag* (Boston) on 1 May 1852, describes a time 'about thirteen years ago, when the now flourishing young city of Hannibal, on the Mississippi River, was but a "wood-yard", surrounded by a few huts, belonging to some hardy "*squatters*", and such a thing as a steamboat was considered quite a sight'. Again in May 1852, in the *American Courier* (Philadelphia) he displayed, in his account of the town, a stock romanticism about noble savages which did not survive into his manhood. ('If the beggar instinct was left out of an Indian,' he

Opposite Above *Home on the Mississippi River by an unknown artist, c. 1865.*
Below *Steamboat Race on the Mississippi after George F. Fuller, 1859*

was to say in *Roughing It*, 'he would not "go" any more than a clock without a pendulum.') Sam Clemens's literary precocity, if one could claim precocity for him, showed itself chiefly in his command of the clichés of trans-Appalachian journalism:

> The first house was built in this city about sixteen years ago. Then the wild war-whoop of the Indian sounded where now rise our stately buildings, and their bark canoes were moored where now land our noble steamers; here they traded their skins for guns, powder, etc. But where now are the children of the forest? Hushed is the war-cry—no more does the light canoe cut the crystal waters of the proud Mississippi; but the remnant of those once power-ful tribes are torn asunder and scattered abroad, and now they wander far, far from the homes of their childhood and the graves of their fathers.
>
> This town is situated on the Mississippi River, about one hundred and thirty miles above St Louis.

The limestone cave, later (as 'McDougal's Cave') the setting for the final episodes of *Tom Sawyer*, was one of the curiosities of Hannibal:

> It is of unknown length; it has innumerable passages, which are not unlike the streets of a large city. The ceiling arches over, and from it hangs beautiful stalactites, which sparkle in the light of the torches, and remind one of the fairy palaces spoken of in the *Arabian Nights*.

Traveling up river in 1838, the year before the Clemens family moved from Florida, the young explorer John Charles Frémont called such small towns as Hannibal 'a sort of fringe to the prairies'. By 1840 Hannibal had a population of a thousand or so, and this tripled by the end of the decade. So far as it 'drowsed', Hannibal drowsed chiefly in Mark Twain's imagination and in the vanished past. By 1844, according to Dixon Wecter, the town had two slaughterhouses, four general stores, three sawmills, two planing mills, three blacksmith shops, two hotels, three saloons, two churches, two schools, a tobacco factory, a hemp factory, and a tanyard, as well as a flourishing distillery. The Mississippi carried the products of this busy port to Louisville and Cincinnati, to St Louis, Memphis, and New Orleans. When gold was found at Sutter's Mill in 1848, some of the villagers packed up and went West, and Hannibal became a main stop on the overland route of the argonauts to St Joseph, Missouri and on to California.

Mark Twain recalled that he and the others boys of his circle 'would have sold our souls to Satan' to have gone to the gold mines, 'that fairy-land of our imagination'. But by the time he said this he had seen the golden age of his boyhood followed by an age which cared about gold only and then by a Gilded Age, which he himself named and in which he

Jane Lampton Clemens, Mark Twain's mother, painted by a travelling artist named Brady in St Louis in 1858 or 1859

Left *In Hannibal, May 1902, in front of the Clemens house on Hill Street.* Right *Entrance to McDowell's Cave ('McDougal's' in* Tom Sawyer*). 'Our last candle burned down to almost nothing before we glimpsed the search party's lights winding about in the distance.'* Autobiography

himself was an eager speculator and participant. He wanted to get rich, not just get along, for money had become Mark Twain's dream, Howells said, 'and he wanted more and more of it to fill out the spaces of this dream'.

But it was Mark Twain the moralist who claimed that 1848 'introduced the change and begot the lust for money which is the rule of life today, and the hardness and cynicism which is the spirit of today'. He looked back on the Californian rush for wealth as a turning point in American morality, the equivalent of the loss of sexual innocence. To know money was to eat of the forbidden tree. In Mark Twain's work, with the chief exception of *Pudd'nhead Wilson*, where he dealt with themes of miscegenation and slavery, money tends to play the role of sex, a process of displacement which may have had its start for him when the gold rush began. For Sam Clemens, as he entered adolescence, was torn between the stern morality of his upbringing and character and such conventional evidences of sexuality along the river as prostitution and concubinage.

Before 1848, the spirit of Hannibal, as he preferred to recall it, was that of a commercial democracy with an 'aristocratic taint', which (along with the institution of slavery) none of the whites there questioned or even recognized as a contradiction. 'The class lines were quite clearly drawn, and the familiar social life of each class was restricted to that class', just as Huck Finn was forbidden company for Tom Sawyer. Yet Hannibal, for all its rigid social structure and its Sabbatarian dourness in the matter of liquor, games and amusements, had a certain communal gaiety. The village took pleasure in circuses, revival meetings, and minstrel shows; in performances by the local Thespians and the Debating Society; in visits from touring ventriloquists, mesmerists, phrenologists, and assorted frauds and scoundrels; in steamboat excursions, parades, torchlight processions, and patriotic holidays celebrated with spread-eagle speeches in the public square, gingerbread in slabs, lemonade, and ice cream. 'Opened with prayer,' Mark Twain noted of one Fourth of July festivity, 'closed with a blessing.'

Hannibal showed its other side to him as well. Sam Clemens remembered pranks and practical jokes brutal enough to unhinge their victims, insanity, the beaten life of squatters and derelicts, hangings, drownings, rapes, lynching, terminal alcoholism, murders. He was eight when he stole into his father's office one night and discovered, lying on the floor in the moonlight, the body of a stabbed man, Hannibal's first recorded homicide. (Judge Clemens was to conduct the coroner's inquest.) He was nine when he witnessed, at noonday, a few yards from the family house, a murder committed in cold anger by one of the town's merchants, later acquitted. Mark Twain recreated the episode in his account of

'There were no public schools in Missouri in those early days, but there were two private schools.' Autobiography

Colonel Sherburn, Boggs, and the cowed lynch mob in Chapter 21 of *Huckleberry Finn*. He witnessed other killings: a slave man struck down with a lump of slag for some trivial offence, perhaps 'for merely doing something awkwardly'; 'a young California emigrant who was stabbed with a bowie knife by a drunken comrade—I saw the red life gush from his breast'; a rowdy stranger from Illinois, also bound for the gold mines, who threatened a widow and was killed by her with a musket (in *Tom Sawyer* this becomes part of Injun Joe's revenge). He remembered, or claimed to remember, in the guilt-seeking way that was to become so central to his character, that early in 1853, six months before he left Hannibal, he gave some matches to a drunken tramp who that night accidentally set fire to his cell in the town jail and burned to death. The tramp 'lay upon my conscience a hundred nights afterwards and filled them with hideous dreams—dreams in which I saw his appealing face as I had seen it in the pathetic reality, pressed against the window bars, with the red hell glowing behind him.'

In Mark Twain's age as well as his youth, such recollections, together with other instances he could cite of inhumanities, humbug, grossness, and treachery, continued to fill his nights with 'hideous dreams'. Sometimes he said he hated the past because it was 'so damned humiliating'. This most desouthernized of Southerners, as Howells called him, was to say, bitterly, that except in the arts of war, murder, and massacre, except for leather-headed anachronisms like duels and tournaments and secondhand imitations of Sir Walter Scott, the South—his South— had contributed nothing of value.

At the three schools he attended in Hannibal until he was about thirteen, young Clemens was a fitful and reluctant student. 'There was not a thing I could do creditably except spell according to the book.' At four and a half he was sent to Mrs Elizabeth Horr, the wife of the village cooper, who with her daughter and two spinster teachers, and for a tuition of twenty-five cents a week for each pupil, taught prayers, the Bible, and McGuffey's Readers. After four years he moved to a common school kept by an Irishman named Cross and then to a new school opened in April 1847 by J. D. Dawson, who appears as the unhappy Mr Dobbins presiding over Tom Sawyer's days and weeks of 'slow suffering in school'. 'The part of my education which I look back upon with the most satisfaction,' Clemens recalled years later, was the 'country school standing in a clearing in the woods' which he attended 'with more or less regularity' during the long summers he spent near Florida, at his

Uncle John Quarles's farm, 'a heavenly place for a boy'. Here, with his wife, eight children, and fifteen or twenty slaves, Quarles, a farmer, lived the self-sufficing, self-supporting agricultural life that was soon to be destroyed by the railroad, industrialism, and the Civil War—it was a way of life that was remembered by some whites as another vanished aspect of the American Eden. 'I can call it all back and make it as real as it ever was, and as blessed,' Mark Twain wrote in his autobiography. 'I can call back the prairie, and its loneliness and peace, and a vast hawk hanging motionless in the sky, with his wings spread wide and the blue of the vault showing through the fringes of their end feathers.' A thousand other images and sensations came back to him—the wail of his aunt's spinning wheel; country feasts of fried chicken, roast pig, fresh venison, pheasant, hot corn pone, peach cobbler; the drowsy dogs blinking in the doorway; a carving knife entering the red heart of a watermelon—'I can see the split fly along in front of the blade as the knife cleaves its way to the other end'; slave stories and speech rhythms that became part of the folk treasure which he preserved by spending it as a writer.

When his father died of pneumonia in 1847, Mark Twain's boyhood came to an end. To contribute to his mother's support, he began a ten-year career as printer, first as an after-school-hours devil in a Hannibal printing office; then as a full-time apprentice for two years; next as Orion's assistant editor and subeditor on his various and invariably ill-fated printing and newspaper ventures in Missouri and Iowa. In June 1853, having first been compelled to swear an oath to his mother that he would stay away from cards and liquor—an oath that, twenty years later, she said had saved him—he set off for St Louis and nearly four years as itinerant typesetter. Half a century later Mark Twain would be an idol of New York society, a fixture along Fifth Avenue and in the city's clubs. But in New York in the summer of 1853 he stayed at a cheap boardinghouse in Duane Street, worked in a printing office in Cliff Street, spent evenings reading in a printers' free library. He was able to assure Jane, 'My promises are faithfully kept.' He saw the Atlantic for the first time, went to the World's Fair at the Crystal Palace on the site of Bryant Park and marveled at the flow of visitors—'6,000 daily;

Overleaf The Country School *by Winslow Homer. 'All the pupils brought their dinners in baskets—corn dodger, buttermilk and other good things.' Auto-biography*

double the population of Hannibal.' 'I have taken a liking to the abominable place,' he said of New York. Nevertheless he moved on, visited Washington, worked at a series of jobs in Philadelphia; Muscatine and Keokuk, Iowa, St Louis, and Cincinnati.

For young Clemens, as for Benjamin Franklin, Abraham Lincoln, Walt Whitman, and countless other Americans, the printing office, together with an itinerant's life, was the poor boy's college; the winds of the world—history, information, ideas, literature of a sort—blew through even the sleepiest provincial establishment, not to mention the composing rooms of the great city papers. It was in the printing office, and in a different way from that of the schoolroom, that Mark Twain said he learned to read and to write. 'One isn't a printer ten years', he said in 1909, 'without setting up acres of good and bad literature, and learning—unconsciously at first, consciously later—to discriminate between the two, within his mental limitations; and meanwhile he is consciously acquiring what is called a "style".' A stray book page that he found blowing down a street in Hannibal, he said, fired his lifelong passion for reading and writing about Joan of Arc and medieval life; of the several versions of *The Mysterious Stranger*, one was set in Hannibal and another in a print shop in fifteenth-century Austria. In a first sighting of his ultimate vocation, Sam Clemens had begun to write occasional newspaper items and correspondence, humorous sketches, a scattering of spoofs, burlesques, and verse, including a poem, 'Love Concealed', to which, in what he later recalled as 'a perfect thunderbolt of humor', he gave the calculatedly provocative dedication, 'To Miss Katie of H——l.' Months later, having by then left for the east, he still relished the confusion of Hell with Hannibal. 'Tell me all that is going on in H——l,' he wrote to Orion from Philadelphia. It was an ambiguity he never fully resolved.

But with the exception of its 'literary feature', life in the printing office was often drudgery. In 1908 he recalled his apprenticeship. 'I worked, not diligently, not willingly, but fretfully, lazily, repiningly, complainingly, disgustedly, and always shirking the work when I was not watched.' Everything he did after those years was play, by contrast. 'I believe I have never done any work since.' The apprentice's job was to build his master's fire in the morning, fetch water from the village pump, sweep the office, wash the rollers, wet and turn the newsprint, set type and later distribute it, work the press, fold the printed newspapers, deliver them in town or envelope and address them for mailing, pursue delinquent subscribers and advertisers—and all this in return for a straw pallet on the office floor at night, meals which were skimpy even on potatoes and turnips, and the promise of two cast-off suits a year.

Washington 1853. Inset *At fifteen, as an apprentice printer*

No longer an apprentice but a journeyman printer, Sam Clemens was still laggard and fretful, and it was clear that typesetting was not to be his vocation—as he told Orion in October 1853, he was slower than the slowest man in the composing room of the Philadelphia *Inquirer*. All his life he maintained a compensating interest in ways of speeding up the process of translating words from the writer's hand to the reader's by way of the printed page. In Washington he had stood before the wood-bed printing press on which Benjamin Franklin had turned out one hundred and twenty-five sheets an hour, and he marveled at the changes a century and a quarter had brought. Now the whirling cylinders of the Hoe press, instrument of a growing democracy and a mass audience, printed twenty thousand sheets in the same time, fast and steady. In time Samuel Clemens, the former printer, became the first author to present his publisher with a typewritten manuscript; he experimented with dictating machines; and he went bankrupt in the attempt to develop, perfect, and market a wondrous machine that would eliminate typesetting by hand.

By the end of 1856 he had become restless in his profession, discouraged by the experience of having worked as Orion's partner in a Keokuk venture that never had any profits to divide. On the strength of a report from South America that 'the native of the mountains of the Madeira region would tramp up and down all day on a pinch of powdered coca and require no other sustenance', he planned to go to the headwaters of the Amazon and open a world trade in this 'vegetable product of miraculous powers', the shrub source of cocaine.

In April 1857, at the age of twenty-one, he boarded the steamer *Paul Jones* at Cincinnati, but before he reached New Orleans on his way to South America and fortune, he changed his mind and persuaded the pilot, Horace Bixby, to take him on as his cub. For five hundred dollars — one hundred dollars down and the rest to be paid out of Clemens' first earnings — Bixby, a veteran pilot who was still on the river in 1912, was to teach him the Mississippi from St Louis to New Orleans, twelve or thirteen hundred miles of points, bends, snags, bars, towheads, crossings, landings, and constant change. Under Bixby, Clemens learned to 'read' the water as he read a book and to know the shape of the river so well

Left *At eighteen, setting out on his travels.* Right 'The City of Memphis *is the largest boat in the trade. . . . I can get a reputation on her.' Letter to Orion, 1859*

Lithograph by E. Sachse & Co., 1855–60. 'The first time I ever saw St Louis I could have bought it for six million dollars and it was the mistake of my life that I did not do it.' Life on the Mississippi

that he could steer at night 'the way you follow a hall at home in the dark. Because you know the shape of it'.

Printing had been only a job, but piloting on the Mississippi, as Sam Clemens had felt since boyhood, was an occupation for heroes. 'I loved the profession far better than any I have followed since, and I took a measureless pride in it.' For in the great days of steamboating before the Civil War the pilot was 'the only unfettered and entirely independent human being that lived in the earth'. Majestic at the wheel, a cigar between his teeth, dressed in fashion like a gentleman, in broadcloth, wearing a gold watch chain, fobs, and a stickpin, the pilot answered to no man. 'I have seen a boy of eighteen taking a great steamer serenely into what seemed almost certain destruction, and the aged captain standing mutely by, filled with apprehension but powerless to interfere.' The pilot was rewarded with absolute authority over his boat when it was under way, with deference, admiring stares, and what for the time

31

was a princely salary—as much as two hundred and fifty dollars a month, which was what the Vice-President of the United States or a Justice of the Supreme Court was getting—and moreover the pilot had no board or lodging to pay while he was on the river.

For dramatic reasons, Mark Twain's account of his education under Bixby, in *Life on the Mississippi*, exaggerated the slowness and callowness of a cub who 'supposed that all a pilot had to do was to keep his boat in the river, and I did not consider that that could be much of a trick, since it was so wide'. In fact, however, he was older, more mature, and more confident than most cubs; he was quick to learn and remember;

Above *The education of a cub pilot. Illustration from* Life on the Mississippi. Opposite *Licensed pilot. 'I took a measureless pride in it. . . . A pilot, in those days was the only unfettered and entirely independent human being that lived in the earth.'* Life on the Mississippi

he was ambitious to become a 'lightning pilot' like Bixby; and he was having a good time. He remembered training under a pilot who liked to declaim Shakespeare while at the wheel and who punctuated his recitations with imprecations and commands:

What man dare, *I* dare!

Approach thou *what* are you laying in the leads for? what a hell of an idea! like the rugged ease her off a little, ease her off! rugged Russian bear,

In accordance with the Act of Congress, approved Aug. 30, 1852.

The Original Renewal

No. 576

PILOT'S CERTIFICATE.

The undersigned, Inspectors for the District of St. Louis, Certify that *Samuel Clemens* having been by them this day duly examined, touching his qualifications as a **Pilot** of a Steam Boat, is a suitable and safe person to be intrusted with the power and duties of Pilot of Steam Boats, and do license him to act as such for one year from this date, on the following rivers, to wit On the Mississippi River to and from St Louis and New Orleans

Given under our hands, this 9th day of April 185 9.

James H. McCord

Wm Singleton

I, James H. McCord, Inspector for the District of St. Louis, certify that the above named Saml Clemens this day, before me, solemnly swore that he would faithfully and honestly, according to his best skill and judgment, without concealment or reservation, perform all the duties required of him as a Pilot, by the Act of Congress, approved August 30, 1852, entitled "An act to amend an act entitled "An act to provide for the better security of the lives of passengers on board of vessels propelled, in whole or in part by steam,' and for other purposes."

Given under my hand, this 9th day of April 185 9.

James H. McCord

Printed by W. S. Haven, Cor. Market & Second Sts. Pittsburgh.

the armed rhinoceros or the *there* she goes! meet her, meet her! didn't you
know she'd smell the reef if you crowded it like that? Hyrcan tiger . . .

('He certainly was a good reader,' Mark Twain said in 1909, 'but it was a
damage to me, because I have never since been able to read Shakespeare
in a calm and sane way.')

Reciprocally, Sam Clemens was entertaining the rivermen with his
own developing kind of humor, including a tale about the 'presence of
mind' he had displayed under pressure when he rescued an old man from
the top of a burning building. 'I yelled for a rope. When it came I threw
the old man the end of it. He caught it and I told him to tie it around his
waist. He did so, and I pulled him down.' And all the while life and experience on the river and ashore in the bustling river cities, their levees
packed solid with steamboats, were opening his eyes to more than the
Mississippi. 'When I find a well-drawn character in fiction or biography,'
he was to say, 'I generally take a warm personal interest in him, for the
reason that I have known him before—met him on the river.'

On 9 April 1859, after two years of apprenticeship, Samuel Clemens
received from the federal inspectors for the District of St Louis a license
as Pilot of Steam Boats. Twenty-one years later, having already published seven major books and written a good part of both *Life on the
Mississippi* and *Huckleberry Finn*, he was to say that if he had his life
to live over again he would 'emerge from boyhood as a "cub pilot" on a
Mississippi boat, and . . . by and by become a pilot, and remain one'—not
an ordinary pilot, but one whom even strangers recognized as 'the
celebrated "Master Pilot of the Mississippi".' 'Master Pilot' is the hero
of a nostalgic fantasy about a life which at other moments he was not
sorry to have left behind him; it is also a metaphor for the literary
eminence of Mark Twain, a name that had come to be so linked with the
river that one of his daughters, hearing the leadsman on a steamer sing
out his soundings, said, 'Don't you know that they are calling for you?'
And 'Mark Twain', like the river itself and like the leadsman's cry
(signifying that the boat was in—whether leaving or entering—twelve
feet of water) suggested danger as well as safe sailing.

'My nightmares to this day', Clemens noted in 1882, 'take the form of
running into an overshadowing bluff, with a steamboat—showing that
my earliest dread made the strongest impression on me.' He remembered
that his brother Henry—'my darling, my pride, my glory, my *all*,' he had

Opposite *The Crystal Palace, New York*

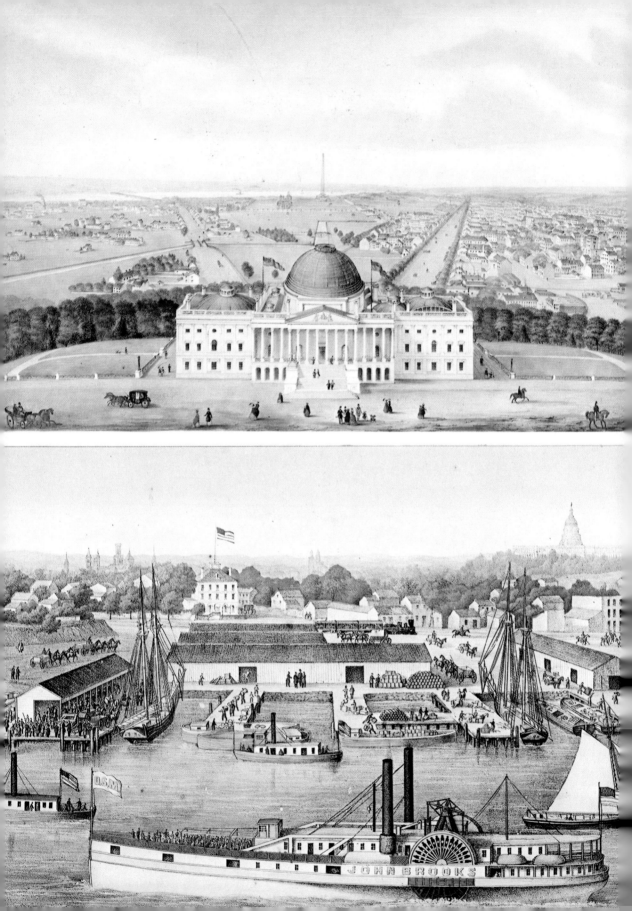

mourned in 1858, praying to be struck dead if this would save the boy—
had been horribly burned when the *Pennsylvania* exploded near
Memphis, an all-too-familiar disaster on the river. He said he was
responsible for the fact that Henry was on that boat, working as a mud
clerk; he also said that he was responsible for the overdose of morphine
that was given him. 'Henry died this morning', he telegraphed a week
after the accident. 'Leave tomorrow with the corpse.' These were other
aspects of piloting on the Mississippi.

Early in 1861, after he had been a licensed pilot for almost two years,
Sam Clemens sent his brother Orion what purported to be an account of
a visit to a New Orleans fortuneteller named Madame Caprell. The
account is so detailed and tendentious that it seems likely that Sam was
using his visit to her as the occasion for one of his frequent, and frequently brutal, attempts to measure his character and potential against
those of his older brother. Orion, the fortuneteller is supposed to have
said,

> never *does* do anything, if he can get anybody else to do it for him; which is
> bad; he never goes steadily on till he attains an object, but nearly always
> drops it when the battle is half won; he is too visionary—he is always flying
> off on a new hobby.

As for Sam at the age of twenty-five:

> I should call yours the best mind, altogether; there is more unswerving
> strength of will and set purpose, and determination and energy in you than
> in all the balance of your family put together.

As if speaking for ambitions in Sam which Sam was not yet willing to
acknowledge to himself, Madame Caprell made a remarkable prophecy:

> Yours is a watery planet; you gain your livelihood on the water; but you
> should have been a lawyer—there is where your talents lie; you might have
> distinguished yourself as an orator, or as an editor; you have written a
> great deal; you write well—but you're rather out of practice; no matter—
> you will be *in* practice some day.

The outbreak of the Civil War two months later sped the fulfillment of
the prophecy. 'The war came,' Clemens later wrote, 'commerce was sus-
pended, my occupation was gone. I had to seek another livelihood.' The
war divided not only the nation but border states like Missouri, families
like the Clemenses, individuals like Sam. 'There was a good deal of

Opposite Above *Washington. Lithograph 1850.* Below *Bird's Eye View of Sixth
Street Wharf, Washington. Lithograph by Chas. Magnus, 1863*

Lithograph by Currier and Ives 1866. Racing on the Mississippi. 'Huzza after huzza thunders from the shores, and the stately creatures go whistling by like the wind.' Life on the Mississippi

confusion in men's minds during the first months of the trouble,' he said in 1885, 'a good deal of unsettledness, of leaning first this way, then that, then the other way.' As a desouthernized Southerner he said this partly in extenuation of his own history and shifting attitudes. On his first visit north in 1853 he had been affronted by the privileges granted Negroes there and mocked, in a letter home, 'I reckon I had better black my face, for in these Eastern states niggers are considerably better than white people.' In April 1861 he was a Southern loyalist, and he gave up his princely occupation on the river in part because he was afraid that he might be forced at pistol point to serve as pilot on a Union gunboat. Orion, though, had been an abolitionist for years, the blackest kind of black Republican, and he remained a loyal Union man. A few days after Abraham Lincoln declared the existence of a state of insurrection, Orion reached the pinnacle of his career. On the recommendation of

Lincoln's Attorney-General, Edward Bates of Missouri, Orion was appointed Secretary of Nevada Territory. This was a position of considerable grandeur, even though Orion found himself hard-put to raise the money to get to Carson City.

Now, contrary to Madame Caprell's—or his own—confident judgments of character and future, it was Sam Clemens who was floundering in direction, who was even literally on the run. In June he saw volunteer military service near Florida as second lieutenant in the Marion Rangers, a band of Confederate militia. 'I was a *soldier* two weeks once in the beginning of the war,' he recalled years later, 'and was hunted like a rat the whole time. Familiar? My splendid Kipling himself hasn't a more burnt-in, hard-baked and unforgettable familiarity with that death-on-the-pale-horse-with-hell-following-after which is a raw soldier's first fortnight in the field—and which, without any doubt, is the most tremendous fortnight and the vividest he is ever going to see.'

After a fortnight of rain, discomfort, boredom, and, above all, growing apprehensions about Union Forces led by an unknown commander named Ulysses Grant, Sam Clemens and the other Marion Rangers said goodbye to each other and to the arts of war and disbanded for the duration. In two weeks in the field he had learned more about retreating, he was to say, 'than the man that invented retreating'. Like Huck Finn, he decided it was time for him to 'light out for the Territory ahead of the rest'.

No longer in the service of the Confederacy, he now became, nominally at least, a recipient of federal patronage and an instrument of federal power, for in July 1861 he started out for Nevada as Orion's private secretary. 'I had become an officer of the government,' he said in *Roughing It*, 'but that was for mere solemnity. The office was a unique sinecure. I had nothing to do and no salary.' With money saved from his pilot's earnings he was able to pay for Orion's stage fare west as well as his own. Among his papers he preserved the receipt for three hundred dollars issued at St Joseph, Missouri, on 25 July 1861, by the Central Overland California and Pike's Peak Express Company—this piece of business paper had proved to be his passport to vocation and another identity.

Chapter Two

Going West: '. . . to excite the *laughter* of God's creatures'
1861–6

They had started west by river steamer, clawing a slow course up the Missouri from St Louis to St Joseph. There they left the States behind them and traveled by stagecoach, 'an imposing cradle on wheels' drawn by six horses, into Nebraska Territory where they saw for the first time prairie-dog villages, antelopes, and coyotes. Entering South Pass, the broad and level valley that crossed the Rockies, they saw banks of snow in the heat of August and, at the Continental Divide, a stream whose waters flowed eastward to the Missouri and the Mississippi and westward to the Gulf of California and the Pacific. After a two-day layover in Salt Lake City the travellers began the final leg of their journey, across Salt Lake Desert and the Great Basin of Nevada to Carson City. This raw territorial capital occupied an impoverished-looking tract of sand, sagebrush, and greasewood surrounded by desolation ('The birds that fly over the land carry their provisions with them,' Sam wrote) and sometimes totally obscured by the Washoe Zephyr, 'a soaring dust drift about the size of the United States set up edgewise'.

By 1871, when Mark Twain was writing about the trip west in *Roughing It*, the American continent had been spanned by rail and what had taken twenty days by lurching stagecoach from St Joseph took barely four days on one of Pullman's Palace Sleeping Cars running on the Union Pacific's Platte Valley Route from Omaha to Oakland. The overland stage had gone into history along with the brief glory of the Pony

Opposite *California News by William S. Mount, 1850. 'The lust for money which is the rule of life today, and the hardness and cynicism which is the spirit of today.'*

Stage Coach Stop by William Hahn

Express rider, 'a little bit of a man, brimful of spirit and endurance', who galloped past the stagecoach 'like a belated fragment of a storm'—

> So sudden is it all, and so like a flash of unreal fancy, that but for the flake of white foam left quivering and perishing on a mail-sack after the vision had flashed by and disappeared, we might have doubted whether we had seen any actual horse and man at all, maybe.

Mark Twain's account of the continental crossing with Orion is a full-throated celebration of a golden era, of travel, youth, adventure, and America's last frontier. 'We felt that there was only one complete and satisfying happiness in the world, and we had found it.' They expected also to find wealth.

In the summer of 1859, miners who for years had been washing spangles of gold out of a blue-black sulfide ore discovered that this ore, which they had been throwing away as otherwise worthless, was worth more than the gold it contained; it was fifteen to twenty percent silver. Soon after, as the news of the discovery spread, the Nevada silver rush brought to the Territory a backwash of the 1849 gold wave into California. Not so long before the sole and uncontested property of the Washoe Indians, the mining camp where silver was found quickly became, as Virginia City, 'the livest town, for its age and population', Clemens said, 'that America ever produced'. Solid lines of wagon traffic moved slowly along Virginia City's principal street, under which stretched 'the

Coming and Going of the Pony Express by Frederick Remington, 1900

opulent length' of the Comstock Lode. That Golconda yielded up vast treasure—six million dollars in silver in 1862, sixteen million dollars in 1864—and would yield up even vaster treasure after 1873, when the Big Bonanza began to be worked. Feverish schemes of wealth—silver, gold, lead, mercury, timber—were in every man's head, and speculation was epidemic.

In the same way the fop journalist Walter Whitman put aside his frock coat and became Walt Whitman, 'one of the roughs', Sam Clemens put aside his river outfits in favor of 'a damaged slouch hat, blue woolen shirt, and pants crammed into boot-tops', and he was on his way toward becoming something other than what he had been. His change of occupation from pilot to Nevada speculator and miner mirrored a shift in the economic climate from the earning of a livelihood to the quest for enormous wealth, the prospect of boom or bust. The mining camps themselves, as he saw them, epitomized a related change, the coming of the plutocracy; out of the Hobbesian turmoil of miners and saloon-keepers, provisioners, speculators, promoters, politicians, and men who worked with picks and shovels, came the lasting divisions of society in the Gilded Age.

Soon after he arrived in the Territory, Sam Clemens went to Lake Tahoe to stake out timber claims. By accident the tenderfoot started a forest fire, saw miles of virgin timberland go up in flames. He was ex-hilarated then by the spectacle of such gorgeous waste ('*Superb!*

43

magnificent! Beautiful!'), and his exhilaration, undiminished by time, spilled over into the gaudy word painting of *Roughing It*:

> Within half an hour all before us was a tossing, blinding tempest of flame! It went surging up adjacent ridges—surmounted them and disappeared in the cañons beyond—burst into view upon higher and farther ridges, presently —shed a grander illumination abroad, and dove again—flamed out again, directly, higher and still higher up the mountainside—threw out skirmishing parties of fire here and there, and sent them trailing their crimson spirals away and among remote ramparts and ribs and gorges, till as far as the eye could reach the lofty mountain-fronts were webbed as it were with a tangled network of red lava streams. Away across the water the crags and domes were lit with a ruddy glare, and the firmament above was a reflected hell!
>
> Every feature of the spectacle was repeated in the glowing mirror of the lake! Both pictures were sublime, both were beautiful; but that in the lake had a bewildering richness about it that enchanted the eye and held it with the stronger fascination.

It seemed that the riches of western Nevada, of the entire country, of Mark Twain's own talents and energies, were as inexhaustible as the great herds of buffalo that roamed the Western plains. Riches were there waiting to be claimed, gathered up, spent, even squandered, as the timber had been squandered and as the gold miners had been squandering their silver ore all those years.

Sam Clemens's timber fever masked only briefly the symptoms of the silver fever that gripped him. While Orion tended to his official duties in Carson City, Sam, acting for both of them, prospected various alluring ventures in the Humboldt and Esmeralda mining districts. 'I've been a prospector and know pay rock from poor when I find it—just with a touch of the tongue,' he wrote in 1890. 'And I've been a silver *miner* and know how to dig and shovel and drill, and put in a blast.' In May 1862 he reported to Orion from Esmeralda: 'I own one eighth of the new "Monitor Ledge, Clemens Company," and money won't buy a foot of it; because I *know* it to contain our fortune.' Their fortune was similarly contained in a bundle of deeds and certificates attesting to ownership of 'feet' and stock in other mines, companies, lodes, and ledges, 'together with all the dips, spurs, and angles, and also all the metals, ores, gold and silver bearing quartz, rock, and earth therein'—the language alone suggests

Opposite Above *Spear Fishing, Lake Tahoe by Albert Bierstadt. 'Three months of camp life on Lake Tahoe would restore an Egyptian mummy to his pristine vigor.'* Roughing It. Below *Saturday Evening in the Mines by Charles Christian Nahl, 1856.* Overleaf *On the Road by Thomas Otter 1860*

that a bonanza was at hand. 'Twelve months, or twenty-four at furthest,' he told Orion, 'will find all our earthly wishes satisfied, so far as money is concerned.' He had decided that he was going to 'make or break here within the next two or three months'. By midsummer, however, he and Orion, hit by assessments on their mining stocks, had reason to suspect that the word for these ventures was not likely to be *bonanza*, but another borrowing from early Mexican prospectors, *borrasca*, meaning 'barren rock, hard luck'.

Orion at least had a salary to fall back on, but Sam was broke and in debt, reduced to shoveling sand in a quartz mine, and beginning to wonder 'how in the h——l' he was going to survive the next few months. 'The fact is, I must have something to do, and that *shortly*, too, even writing.' To earn his board, he told Orion, he was willing to do any amount of correspondence for whoever would have him, the Sacramento *Union* or the Carson City *Silver Age*. At the end of July 1862 he received from the Virginia City *Territorial Enterprise*, to which he had already contributed sketches and letters, the offer of a job as local reporter at twenty-five dollars a week. Before he made up his mind to accept, more than a week had passed; before he left Esmeralda for Virginia City, more than a month had passed. It was neither the first nor the last time in his life that he experienced the bitter cycle of boom and bust, prospective wealth and present desperation. Nor was it the last time that, casually, passively, even reluctantly, he allowed himself to be turned toward authorship.

Even rivals like the Gold Hill *Daily News* conceded that the *Enterprise* was the Territory's leading paper. Its editor, Joseph T. Goodman, and its star writer, Dan De Quille (the pseudonym of William Wright), were far out of the ordinary run of Western journalists. Toward the end of a restless career Goodman became an acknowledged authority on Mayan archaeology and inscriptions, while in 1876, largely at the instigation of his friend and former pupil, Samuel Clemens, Dan De Quille published *The Big Bonanza*, a basic source book for Comstock history.

Trained by them as a news, or city, reporter, but at the same time

Opposite *Gold Mining in California. Lithograph by Currier and Ives, 1871*

Overleaf *Virginia City. Lithograph after Grafton T. Brown, 1861. 'Under it was another busy city . . . where a great population of men thronged in and out among an intricate mass of tunnels and drifts.'* Roughing It

J. DRAKES CARPENTER SHOP.

OFFICE OF THE TERRITORIAL ENTERPRISE.

J. WILLIAMS & CO.

RESIDENCE OF M. H. BRYAN.

CIGARS, TOBACCO, STATIONARY & FANCY GOODS. J. S. BLOOMFIELD & CO.

LOUIS FEUSIER.

FLORA TEMPLE LIVERY. J. H. GARDINER.

TUNNEL OF THE MT. DAVIDSON G. & S. MINING CO.

BLACKSMITHING & WAGON SHOP. WILLARD & EELLS, PRO.

PAVILION. JOHN L. MOORE, PP.

RESIDENCE OF JNO. A. COLLINS.

MAIN ENTRANCE TO VIRGINIA CITY.

A. FLEISHHACKER & CO.

BLACK & HOWELL. PROVISIONS HARDWARE GROCERIES & LIQUORS.

L. HERMANN.

RESIDENCE OF O. MALDONADO.

BEYREUTHERS BUILDING. PIONEER DRUG STORE. LANGTONS EXPRESS. Dr. E. SMITH. NELSON W. WINTON, AGENT.

Left *Fire at Lake Tahoe. Illustration from* Roughing It. Right *Gold Hill, Nevada, by an unknown artist, 1862*

liberated by the paper's boisterous, satiric spirit, Clemens followed his own natural bent. In October he published the first of several notoriously successful hoaxes he was to write for the *Enterprise*. This sober and circumstantial news story dealt with the discovery, at Gravelly Ford, of a petrified man who, according to the coroner's inquest, had died of 'protracted exposure' more than three hundred years ago; the corpse who could now be given a Christian burial only with the aid of blasting powder to dislodge it from a seated position in which, if one carefully pieced together the scattered details of the description, it had been thumbing its nose. Clemens was in part paying off a personal grudge against the new coroner and justice of the peace of Humboldt, just as in his next hoax, 'The Empire City Massacre', he dealt with the iniquitous corporate practice of declaring 'cooked', or false, dividends in order to inflate the price of stocks. According to Clemens's imagined, credible, and horribly gripping report, a speculator named P. Hopkins (there was, in actuality, a Peter Hopkins, well-known bachelor and proprietor of the Magnolia Saloon in Carson City) had been victimized by a cooked-dividend fraud, went berserk, massacred his wife and six of his children; then he

> dashed into Carson on horseback, with his throat cut from ear to ear, and bearing in his hand a reeking scalp, from which the warm, smoking blood was still dripping, and fell in a dying condition in front of the Magnolia saloon. Hopkins expired, in the course of five minutes, without speaking.

Left *Around thirty, reporter in San Francisco.* Right *Composing room of the Virginia City* Territorial Enterprise

'It was the talk of the town, it was the talk of the Territory,' Clemens recalled of his hoax. 'Most of the citizens dropped gently into it at breakfast, and they never finished their meal. There was something about those minutely faithful details that was a sufficing substitute for food.' In such practical jokes, and in his other writing for the *Enterprise*, Clemens was developing a style of personal, fantastic journalism which was often motivated by affront and outrage as much as by the desire to entertain. Just as he had paid back the Humboldt coroner he undertook to dispose of the editor of the Carson *Independent* who, more than a year after 'The Empire City Massacre', was still publicly scolding its author. Clemens responded:

> It is my unsolicited opinion that he knows very little about anything. And anybody who will read his paper calmly and dispassionately for a week will endorse that opinion. And more especially his knowing nothing about Carson, is not surprising; he seldom mentions that town in his paper. If the Second Advent were to occur here, you would hear of it first in some other newspaper.

On 3 February 1863, six months after Clemens joined the *Enterprise*, a new comic name and identity—soon to become complex, demanding, and historical—made its first recorded appearance. A humorous travel letter to the *Enterprise*, datelined Carson City, was signed, 'Yours, dreamily, Mark Twain.' Years later Clemens was to say that he had borrowed the name, in tribute and amends, from an old pilot he had once satirized in print, 'Isaiah Sellers, who used to write river news over it for the New Orleans *Picayune*', but no one has ever been able to confirm that account or to remove the powerful suspicion that Clemens either invented or misremembered the story. Moreover, the traditional belief that 'Mark Twain' derived from the leadsman's term for two fathoms has even been disputed by evidence which suggests that the name originated not on the Mississippi but in Nevada, where it may have been associated by saloonkeepers with a common practice of marking up two drinks on credit. The tissue of fiction and ambiguity that sur-rounds the origin of the name does not stop there.* His friend Howells preferred to call him Clemens 'instead of Mark Twain, which seemed always somehow to mask him from my personal sense'. On the other hand, George Bernard Shaw, a professional at public identities, pre-ferred 'Mark Twain'—'I have always regarded Clemens as mere material; might have been your brother or your uncle.' He is 'Mark' to old jour-nalism and lecturing friends, 'Twain' to others, 'Clemens' to many more; his wife found it difficult to call him 'Sam', which is the name his family and Hannibal friends used; and he himself often solved the problem by signing the double autograph, 'Samuel L. Clemens Mark Twain'. Yet, despite the murky history of the name, the opening sentence of Mark Twain's travel letter from Carson City has the overtones of a great personal discovery, the end of a moratorium. 'I feel very much as if I had just awakened from a long sleep.' The writer, the former printer, pilot, speculator, and prospector, was twenty-seven years old.

Rubbing the sleep from his eyes, Mark Twain, with increasing freedom and confidence, wrote local news, personal satire, journalistic horseplay, comic libels, occasional editorials, travel correspondence from Steam-boat Springs and from his frequent trips to San Francisco, and, from Carson City, legislative reports and reports of the Constitutional Con-vention of 1863. 'I am prone to boast', he wrote to his mother and Pamela after less than a year on the *Enterprise*, 'of having the widest reputation, as a local editor, of any man on the Pacific Coast.' But already he felt the stirrings of a national consciousness and a national ambition. Visiting San Francisco in May 1863 he walked down Montgomery Street like a celebrity—it was as full of familiar faces as Main Street in

---

* 'If we are not sure about the origin of the name and its meaning, we are equally in doubt about what name to use in writing about the man. . . . The uncertainty fully manifests itself in indexes, where three possibilities—"Clemens," "Mark Twain," and „Twain, Mark"—must be checked if one is to be *sure* of Mark Twain's absence.' (James M. Cox, *Mark Twain: The Fate of Humor* [Princeton, N.J.: Princeton University Press, 1966], p. 23.)

Hannibal—and he went to the Cliff House to watch the sea lions and the ships passing, to listen to the roar of the surf, and to wet his feet in the Pacific as he had wet them in the Atlantic ten years earlier: 'I had a proper appreciation of the vastness of this country—for I had traveled from ocean to ocean across it.' Enlarged in consciousness, inquiring, tireless, like Walt Whitman he faced west from California's shores, and soon he was to make plans to go westward around the world by way of the Hawaiian Islands and China.

Meanwhile admonitions of gentility and piety were reaching him from home; he was still accountable. He did his best to convince his mother and sister that he moved only in 'the best Society' of Virginia City and San Francisco and that he actually had 'a *reputation* to

The Cliff House, San Francisco. Lithograph by Currier and Ives

Left *Artemus Ward, prince of platform entertainers. 'I wish him well, and a safe journey, drunk or sober.'* Territorial Enterprise, *1864.* Centre *Dan De Quille (William Wright) of the* Territorial Enterprise *and historian of the Comstock Lode.* Right *Ambrose Bierce, journalist, author, and celebrity of San Francisco's literary frontier, by J. H. E. Parkington*

preserve'. But in truth he had become a prominent part of the Pacific Slope's gaudy subculture of writers, reporters, entertainers, traveling actors, and short-term promoters, and he was to look back on such times as these with nostalgia, as part of 'that old day when bohemianism was respectable—ah, more than respectable, heroic'. As he later confessed to his future mother-in-law, he had been 'a man of convivial ways and not averse to social drinking'. He had marked up many more than two drinks on credit and claimed to have observed an extraordinary meteoric shower through two telescopic glass tumblers, washed out frequently with *eau de vie* and Veuve Cliquot. 'Some of the finest intellects of the day have been blunted by liquor,' Artemus Ward, the premier humorist of the day, joked to Clemens after the marathon Christmas Eve they celebrated together in 1863 at Barnum's Restaurant in Virginia City. The evening ended, Clemens recalled, with himself, Goodman, and Dan De Quille slumped at the table while Artemus Ward thickly proposed a 'stanning' toast. 'Well,' Ward said, after an honest but futile attempt to rise to his feet, '*consider* it stanning.'

Sam Clemens' career on the *Enterprise* was brought to an end by a curious episode. It illustrates the freewheeling character of Nevada journalism, his characteristic response to its challenge, and his equally characteristic way of reshaping his own history and approximating the liberties of fiction. In an editorial published in May 1864, a month when Grant was fighting the bloody battles of the Wilderness and Spottsylvania and Sherman was marching through Georgia, Clemens suggested, in the vein of his other hoaxes, that money raised by the ladies of Carson City for the relief of sick and wounded Union soldiers was actually being diverted to 'aid a Miscegenation Society somewhere in the East'. He was referring to a miscegenation rumor that was used against the Republican Party in 1864, but even so the reference was a blunder in taste and tact— Virginia City had a hard enough time during the war living down its reputation as a sanctuary for Copperheads and Secessionists. As he explained to Orion's wife (one of the now aggrieved ladies of Carson City), he had written the item and laid it before Dan De Quille as a private joke, 'when I was not sober'. Neither of them intended the editorial for print, and Clemens had left his manuscript on the table. 'I suppose the foreman, prospecting for copy, found it, and seeing that it was in my

Devil's Gate. Stagecoach from Virginia City passes the toll house en route *to Gold Hill and Silver City*

handwriting, thought it was to be published, and carried it off.' Now Clemens was in a corner: he could not exonerate himself 'by saying the affair was a silly joke, and that I and all concerned were drunk. No— I'll die first.' He was willing to have the ladies appoint someone to avenge them on the field of honor.

In *Roughing It* Mark Twain said he left Nevada because he had spring fever and also because he was suddenly presented with an opportunity to go to New York and promote a rich silver mine which had just been discovered. Much later, in his autobiography, he said that in the outcry that followed the 'miscegenation' editorial, he had accepted a challenge from James L. Laird, one of the proprietors of the Virginia City *Daily Union*, and that they agreed to fight it out with Colt navy revolvers; that through a picturesque misunderstanding which involved a small bird killed from a distance of thirty yards Laird conceived an erroneous notion of Clemens's marksmanship and fled the field of honor; and that in any case, because of an antidueling statute then in force, Clemens had to leave the Territory in order to escape imprisonment. Challenges were in fact exchanged; but, aside from that, the silver mine Clemens was supposed to promote in New York appears to have been as pure an invention as the antidueling statute. The episode of the dead bird and the rival's retreat is borrowed whole from a popular comic story. Clemens left Nevada, it now seems clear, because it was suicide for a humorist to make a public fool of himself. The 'miscegenation' fiasco, compounded of accident, intention, and a degree of truth as well as of demonic (or alcoholic) possession, is related to other mortifying instances sprinkled through Mark Twain's life and subject to 'correction' as well as regret.*

He was on the run again, first, in May 1864, from Virginia City to San Francisco, where he worked, unhappily, as a reporter on the *Morning Call*; then, in December, he went to the Mother Lode hills of California in Tuolumne and Calaveras counties. For a while he lived in a rude cabin on Jackass Hill and tried to scratch out a living as a pocket miner

---

* Far from being a casual topic, miscegenation appears to have been a good deal on Clemens's mind throughout his life. As a young printer's apprentice he understood that by the customs of slave-holding societies, it was a man's right to make love to a black girl 'if he wanted to'. But he also understood the taboo that was a corollary of this: that by the same 'customs' the swiftest and most brutal retribution would come to any black man who exercised this 'right' with a white woman. Clemens reported that in New York in 1869 he saw Edwin Booth as Iago in Shakespeare's play about 'the great Miscegenationist'. Miscegenation was a central topic of *Pudd'nhead Wilson* (1894) and of a remarkable dream that Clemens recorded in detail in his notebook early in 1897 (see page 169). An allied concern: in a notebook of 1885 he predicted that the next one hundred years would bring black supremacy to America—'whites under foot' (Mark Twain Papers, University of California Library, Berkeley.)

'in the one little patch of ground in the whole globe where Nature conceals gold in pockets', he recalled years later. 'One gleam of jollity' relieved an otherwise dismal and defeated winter of mud, rain, and meals of dishwater and beans. Around the saloon stove in Angel's Camp he heard, for the first time in his experience, a Western analogue of an ancient tale, and he summarized it in his notebook:

> Coleman with his jumping frog—bet a stranger $50.—Stranger had no frog and C. got him one:—In the meantime stranger filled C's frog full of shot and he couldn't jump. The stranger's frog won.

This story, in its raw form no more than 'a villainous backwoods sketch', as he said, was 'the germ of my coming good fortune', for it was the germ of the story he wrote and sent East, on the advice of Artemus Ward, as 'Jim Smiley and His Jumping Frog'. It was published in the New York *Saturday Press* on 18 November 1865, and soon after, through the newspaper exchanges, the frog, if not yet its author, became celebrated across the country. A complex and completely controlled story, the 'Jumping Frog' is the dazzling landmark of Mark Twain's early career and a model for some of the best of his later work—the oral, humorous, first-person story rendered in print, a work of 'high and delicate art' which relies for its effectiveness on the manner of the telling, digressions and all, instead of on the outcome, is delivered gravely and unsuspectingly, with no cues for laughter or acknowledgment of the ludicrous. It 'may be spun out to great length, and may wander around as much as it pleases, and arrive nowhere in particular'.*

All of this applies to the 'Jumping Frog' and to the people who, through various kinds of interplay, come miraculously to life in it: good-natured, garrulous old Simon Wheeler, who wears an 'expression of winning gentleness and simplicity upon his tranquil countenance' and never betrays 'the slightest suspicion of enthusiasm' or the slightest hint that there was anything 'ridiculous or funny about his story'; Jim Smiley, ever hopeful and trusting, always betting; the stranger who says, with calculated challenge, 'Well, *I* don't see no p'ints about that frog that's any better'n any other frog'; and Mark Twain, the bookish narrator who listens with imperturbable boredom to Wheeler's wonderful stories and transcribes them dutifully. 'Between you and I, privately, Livy dear,' Clemens was to say to his fiancée in December 1869, 'it is the

---

* Writing in the *Golden Era* (San Francisco) on 26 June 1864, Clemens had articulated this standard in his account of a favorite Washoe comedian, Fred Franks, who possessed 'the first virtue of a comedian, which is to do humorous things with grave decorum and without seeming to know that they are funny'. (Reprinted in Edgar M. Branch, ed., *Clemens of the Call.* Berkeley and Los Angeles: University of California Press, 1969, p. 40.)

best humorous sketch America has produced yet, and I must read it in public some day, in order that people may know what there is in it.'

Nearing the age of thirty, a familiar watershed time for self-redefinition (in their early thirties Jesus set out on his ministry and Luther nailed his theses to the church door), Samuel Clemens made his own significant departures. He began to explore the literary and psychological options of Mark Twain, the identity he created as a means of liberating and extending himself. Already savoring the praise of 'editors of standard literary papers in the distant east' but nevertheless harried, in debt, working desperately hard to get out of debt, he sent Orion, from San Francisco on 19 October 1865, a remarkable letter of purpose, summing-up, and apology:

> I never had but two *powerful* ambitions in my life. One was to be a pilot, & the other a preacher of the gospel. I accomplished the one and failed in the other, *because* I could not supply myself with the necessary stock in trade—*i.e.*, religion. I have given it up forever.... But I have had a 'call' to literature, of a low order—*i.e.*, humorous. It is nothing to be proud of, but it is my strongest suit, & if I were to listen to that maxim of stern duty which says that to do right you must multiply the one or the two or the three talents which the Almighty trusts to your keeping, I would long ago have ceased to meddle with the things for which I was by nature unfitted & turned my attention to seriously scribbling to excite the *laughter* of God's creatures. Poor, pitiful business! Though the Almighty did his part by me—for the talent is a mighty engine when supplied with the steam of education—which I have not got, & so its pistons and cylinders & shafts move feebly & for a holiday show & are useless for any good purpose.*

He wanted to strike a bargain with Orion, who had been passed over for office the year before when Nevada became a state and now seemed to be drifting again: Sam would apply himself to exciting the laughter of God's creatures if Orion would apply himself to any one rational and realistic pursuit. 'You had better shove this in the stove,' he said at the end of his letter, in ironic reference to the seriousness of his 'call'—'I don't want any "absurd literary remains" & "unpublished letters of Mark Twain" published after I am planted', which is, of course, exactly what happened.

'I am generally placed at the head of my breed of scribblers in this part of the country,' Sam told his mother in January 1866; the 'Jumping Frog,' reprinted in *The Californian*, a literary journal, had consolidated his reputation on the Coast. But at the same time he freely conceded that

---

* Published in *The Berkeley Albion* (1961).

the place of eminence 'properly belongs to Bret Harte'. Harte was a year younger than Clemens, but he had found his literary vocation so early, brilliantly, and commandingly that he seemed less a contemporary than a mentor and an eminence. Recognizing a dominant and competing nature in Clemens, Harte managed to maintain, for his own protection, a certain condescending air, a mocking tone, the superiority of the

Riding the Jumping Frog to fame

dandy, and the authority of a master over his pupil. In order to free him for writing, Harte had been provided with a relatively undemanding job in the United States Mint, and he was the acknowledged leader of a group which included among its major figures Mark Twain, Ambrose Bierce, and Henry George, the future author of *Progress and Poverty*, and among its minor celebrities Ina Coolbrith, Charles Warren Stoddard, Joaquin Miller, and Charles Henry Webb, the owner and editor of the

Californian. During the two years (1868–70) of Bret Harte's brilliant editorship, the *Overland Monthly* was to become the *Atlantic* of the Pacific Coast, evidence of a literary culture and a literary frontier that had a vitality all their own, altogether different from the decorum and high-mindedness of New England. In time Clemens was to feud bitterly with Bret Harte, as he also did with Webb, but at this point, and in 1868 when he was in San Francisco again and writing *The Innocents Abroad*, he deferred to Harte and eagerly learned from him. Later he acknowledged that Harte 'trimmed and trained and schooled me patiently, until he changed me from an awkward utterer of coarse grotesquenesses to a writer of paragraphs and chapters that have found a certain favor in the eyes of even some of the very decentest people in the land'.

Despite his own growing reputation and his acceptance into Bret Harte's innermost circle, Clemens found that life in San Francisco and along the Coast was full of queer vicissitudes. One day might find him with two new suits to his name, twelve hundred dollars in the bank, and no debts, living high on oysters, salmon, cold fowl, and champagne at the Occidental Hotel, which he celebrated as 'Heaven on the half shell'. The next day might see him down and out, by necessity an expert at skulking and dodging, unpopular with the police because he said they were brutal and corrupt. At one point he even found himself in jail charged with drunkenness, and this was probably a warning from the police of worse things to come.

During a low period in 1866 he put a pistol to his head, and forty years later, having since decided that 'Pity is for the living, envy is for the dead', he reflected: 'Many times I have been sorry I did not succeed, but I was never ashamed of having tried.' During the same low period, in February 1866, an editor on the Gold Hill (Nevada) *News* described him in print as a 'Bohemian from the sagebrush', a jailbird, bail-jumper, deadbeat, and alcoholic who, the writer insinuated, had been rolled in a whorehouse and probably had a venereal disease—he would not be missed in the city by the Golden Gate. Even for an era of scurrilous personal journalism, this was a frightful attack. Clemens's answer was to depart in silence, as correspondent, at twenty dollars for each weekly dispatch, for the Sacramento *Union*, the most powerful paper in the West. In March 1866 he sailed on the steamer *Ajax* for what years later he still recalled, in relief, as paradise, the kingdom of Hawaii.

Clemens scored a dramatic scoop in a dispatch that he sent to the *Union* from Honolulu on 25 June, an account of the burning at sea of the clipper ship *Hornet*; it was based on interviews with survivors who had reached Laupahoehoe in an open boat after forty-three days of hunger, exposure, delirium, and the threat of cannibalism. This dispatch to the

Union, widely reprinted and talked about, brought him a new kind of fame, as a straight news reporter, and in the hope of parlaying this fame into something more literary he reworked the *Hornet* story, as 'Forty-three Days in an Open Boat', for the December 1866 issue of *Harper's New Monthly Magazine*. He preferred to think of this first appearance in a genteel Eastern journal as 'my literary début', even though the début was marred by his mortifying discovery that the magazine listed him as 'Mark Swain'.

For the most part, Clemens's five months away from San Francisco were a period of consolidation, of sifting the possibilities inherent in his pseudonym. In letters to the *Union* he had begun to develop a new character, 'Mr Brown'. Contrasted with the gentlemanly, bookish, and solemn Mark Twain, Brown was the savage American, rebellious, derisive, colloquial, a bachelor on the loose with an eye for drink and women. 'Brown had a couple of peanuts for lunch,' Mark Twain reported, 'and therefore one could not say that he was full of whiskey, without shamefully transcending the limits of truth.' In time this raffish *Doppelgänger* would be reabsorbed into Mark Twain, who would thereby acquire a greater range of mood and stance and grow nearer to becoming a fully rounded literary persona. The notebooks Clemens kept contain various exchanges between Mark Twain and Mr Brown.

Left *Bret Harte*. Right *Honolulu harbor, Island of Oahu. The natives 'will lie for a dollar when they could get a dollar and a half for telling the truth'. Lecture, 1866*

They also contain evidences that Clemens was taking a new view of his materials as a writer.

At sea seventeen hundred miles west of San Francisco he saw his first twilight since leaving Missouri five years earlier ('No twilight in the Islands, California, or Washoe'); his thoughts were turning homeward, backward in time. He recalled the dead man he found lying in the moonlight on the floor of his father's office in Hannibal. He made notes for the cat-and-painkiller episode that was to become Chapter 12 of *Tom Sawyer*. He listed some of the superstitions that would play a part in his Hannibal novels: how you removed freckles by washing your face in rainwater; how you could transfer your warts to another boy; how a slave ties a thread in his hair to keep witches away.

At the same time he was recovering the present as well as the past. The war was over, and Samuel Clemens, a reconstructed Southerner who had gone West to find that his ambitions were national, now reminded himself that one of the secrets of eloquence was simplicity, as he had learned from studying Abraham Lincoln's speech of purpose and reconciliation—'with malice toward none; with charity for all. . . .' The former Marion Ranger now cited with admiration the eloquent simplicity of General Grant's message to Buckner at Fort Donelson, 'I propose to move immediately upon your works.' Twenty years later, as Grant's friend and publisher, Clemens was to rise to a new level of purple eloquence and indignation when he defended the simple prose of this 'simple soldier, who, all untaught of the silken phrase-makers, linked words together with an art surpassing the art of the schools and put into them a something which will still bring to American ears, as long as America shall last, the roll of his vanished drums and the tread of his marching hosts'.

Eloquence of this sort rather than Grant's or Lincoln's lay near the heart of Clemens's first venture, and first success, as a popular lecturer soon after his return to San Francisco. His subject was the Sandwich Islands, and along with humor and an antic, drawling, shuffling style of delivery, he regaled his hearers with gorgeous word paintings of Kilauea in eruption, passages of sublime, gaudy, purple description. At Maguire's Academy of Music, on Pine Street, on 2 October 1866, he had a seizure of stage fright so intense that he saw the face of death, but then he discovered a kind of triumph that he was always to find intoxicating, addictive. He found himself the master of his audience, and at his will he could make it laugh or applaud or gasp in wonderment—'Be them your natural tones of eloquence?' He had learned much from his friend Artemus Ward, the prince of platform entertainers; he still had much to learn, and for years he would be compared with Ward; but he already

Steamship leaving San Francisco

had a style and presence that were altogether his own, that delighted his audience in San Francisco, and, as he went on tour that fall, delighted other audiences in Sacramento, Grass Valley, Red Dog, You Bet, and Gold Hill.

Even with these victories he had begun to feel confined by the Coast. After the freedom of Hawaii and the expanses of the Pacific, San Francisco no longer seemed home to him but 'prison'. With a new commission as traveling correspondent, this time from the *Alta California* of San Francisco, he planned to go to the Paris Exposition. But first it was time to see the States again, to go to New York, see his mother in St Louis, and then go abroad. In bright sunlight, on 15 December 1866, he sailed from San Francisco on the sidewheeler *America*.

Chapter Three

Going East: 'Make your mark . . .'
1867–71

Samuel Clemens was thirty-one when he arrived in New York in January 1867. He had as yet made no binding commitment to place or social identity. But within three miraculous years the tramp journalist and 'Wild Humorist of the Pacific Slope' became, in his publisher's description, 'The People's Author', and he also began to win official literary recognition. 'The Bohemian from the sagebrush' married into Eastern wealth and status, became a gentleman and a newspaper owner, and—a far cry from his cabin on Jackass Hill—lived in a brownstone mansion and was driven about in his own carriage by a liveried coachman. Mark Twain's success was to shape the dreams of young authors setting out to conquer America. Later on, his satisfaction would be eroded by the feeling that part of the price for whirlwind triumph had to be anger, a divided heart, and a muted voice. But in the flow of these changes Clemens thought of himself as 'Little Sammy in Fairyland' who lived in an Aladdin's palace. Later he liked to tell and retell what his friend Howells called 'the inexhaustible, the fairy, the Arabian Nights story' of his life.

His base for this spring into a new life was New York. 'Make your mark in New York,' he soon reported, with a prophetic play on words, 'and you are a made man. With a New York endorsement you may travel the country over, without fear—but without it you are speculating upon a dangerous issue.' The war had made New York the scrambling center of American life. 'There is something about this ceaseless buzz, and hurry, and bustle', Clemens reported, 'that keeps a stranger in a

Opposite Fifth Avenue, New York. The twin-spired building on the left is Temple Emanu-El, 1868

state of unwholesome excitement all the time, and makes him restless and uneasy, and saps from him all capacity to enjoy anything or take a strong interest in any matter whatever—a something which impels him to try to do everything, and yet permits him to do nothing. He is a boy in a candy-shop.'

Shipping center, hive of trade and manufacture, the city ruled the nation's finance, fashion, manners, and ideas, and it fed the nation's hunger for print. New York focused the energies, aspirations, and standards of a new mass audience, whose spokesman and hero Mark Twain was to become. His interests, like theirs, were not in high culture of the sort generally associated with New England, but in a relatively new area bounded by journalism, humor, entertainment, and popular literature, and characterized, if one were successful, less by status than by celebrity and abundant cash crops.

'Honest poverty is a gem that even a king might feel proud to call his own, but I wish to sell out. I have sported that kind of jewelry long enough.' So the traveling correspondent of the *Alta California* reported to his readers back in San Francisco. He also reported to them on the sights and celebrities of the city, its renowned extremes of squalor and splendor, shadow and sunshine: the slums and criminal nests of the Lower East Side and the mansions of the very rich on Fifth Avenue; Harry Hill's Bowery rumhole and the august Century Association; the police lockup (where Clemens spent a night for street brawling) and the fashionable churches where godliness and prosperity went hand in hand, their union blessed by doctrine and preachment, and where he heard the Reverend Henry Ward Beecher fire off pulpit pyrotechnics that left him dazzled, with a nearly overwhelming impulse to applaud. Briefly, but with a certain symbolic weight, he reported on the passage through New York City of Jefferson Davis, just freed from a federal prison, and of the body of Artemus Ward, dead at thirty-three and leaving vacant a place in popular entertainment that Mark Twain, his friend and protégé, could soon claim.

A trip home in March 1867, after an absence of six years, only re-inforced his belief that the East was where he belonged. Years earlier he vowed that he would not look upon his mother's face again, or Pamela's, 'until I am a rich man'. He had made a certain name, but no fortune yet, and now in St Louis, where his family lived, he felt reproach in the air, his own and theirs. But in St Louis, nevertheless, on 25 March, he tasted victory again on the stage, talking about the Sandwich Islands and giving a performance quite different from anyone else's on the lecture circuit. He delighted his audience with a mixture of statistics and anecdotes, edification and amusement, humorous reflections delivered

after a delicately timed pause, something that passed for moral philosophy, and passages of gorgeous word painting. '*Any* lecture of mine', he
was to say a few years later, 'ought to be a running narrative-plank, with
square holes in it, six inches apart, all the length of it, and then in my
mental shop I ought to have plugs (half marked "serious" and the other
marked "humorous") to select from and jam into these holes according
to the temper of the audience.' And as for that temper, he was soon to
demonstrate that he could judge it with awesome accuracy and even
possess his audience by the sheer force of his personality. 'No man will
dare more than I to get it,' he said of such conquests.

A week later he lectured in Hannibal, now fallen on hard times. The
railroads had taken away its river traffic, and the town was in danger of
becoming the drowsing hamlet he preferred to remember from his boyhood. Like the cannon fire which was supposed to release the bodies of
Tom and Huck from the river bottom, the brief visit sent a few connected
images of the past floating up to his consciousness. He recalled, and
probably for the first time in print wrote about, 'Jimmy Finn', the town
drunkard, who for a while was won over by the temperance people, 'but
in an evil hour temptation came upon him, and he sold his body to a
doctor for a quart of whiskey, and that ended all his earthly troubles.
He drank it all at one sitting, and his soul went to its long account and
his body went to Dr Grant.' He remembered that he himself, for the sake
of a stunning red scarf, had once joined the Cadets of Temperance and
pledged himself not to drink, smoke, or swear; after four months, during
which there were no funeral processions he could march in to show off
his scarf, he resigned, and within the next three weeks 'pretty nearly all
the distinguished citizens in the camp died'.

From Hannibal he went north to Keokuk, before the war a gate city
to the headlands of the Mississippi and now, like Hannibal, in a trough
between waves of expansion and speculation. Eleven years before, he
had worked in Orion's print shop there. Now he spent the weekend in
Keokuk's fashionable hotel, a visiting celebrity greeted by posters
which announced a lecture to be given by 'Sam. Clemens, the greatest
humorist in America'. The newspapers welcomed 'the most extraordinary delineator of human character in America or upon the continent of Europe'. He was at ease in his lecture to a bigger house than
Emerson had drawn, and he was happy and playful. Seeing an old friend
in the audience, he qualified his description of a Hawaiian ruler: 'One
of the greatest liars on the face of the earth, except one, and I am very
sorry to locate that one right here in Keokuk, in the person of Ed
Brownell.' Another lecture in Quincy, Illinois, and then he started on
the return trip to New York. The farther he got from home the more

The 9:45 a.m. Accommodation, Stratford, Connecticut by Edward L. Henry, 1867

attractive the fields and cities of the republic seemed as he looked at them from the express. What he saw now was not the black pall that had hung over Pittsburgh on the trip west, but, all the way through Ohio and New Jersey, wonderful cities, 'so cheerful and handsomely built, and so fiercely busy. It is good to come to the States occasionally, and see what a great country it is.'

In New York again, he looked beyond his regular correspondence to three ventures that promised to help him make his 'mark'. At the end of April 1867 he brought out his first book, *The Celebrated Jumping Frog of Calaveras County and Other Sketches*, edited by his friend Webb and with a preface introducing Mark Twain, 'Wild Humorist of the Pacific Slope' and 'Moralist of the Main', as an author 'too well known to the public to require a formal introduction', and one who, unlike other humorists—Webb had in mind Artemus Ward, Petroleum V. Nasby, and Josh Billings—did not have to resort to tricks of spelling or 'rhetorical buffoonery'. Soon Clemens reported jauntily, and hopefully, to his

California newspaper readers that the book was handsome, readable, and selling well (this last claim, at any rate, was remote from the truth). It was in another vein altogether that he told Bret Harte about the new book: 'It is full of damnable errors of grammar and deadly inconsistencies of spelling in the frog sketch, because I was away and did not read the proofs.'

On 6 May, spurred on by the entrepreneurial enthusiasm of another Western friend, Frank Fuller, a wartime Governor of Utah Territory, Clemens made his New York début as a lecturer in the Great Hall of Cooper Union. Like the book, the lecture was a financial failure— Fuller packed the house with schoolteachers on complimentary tickets. But it was an investment in the future, a critical and strategic victory. The New York reviews, appreciative and influential, were copied in other cities and towns and helped establish Mark Twain as one of the new stars of the lecture circuit. Soon he was able to turn down lecture invitations from all over and bide his time until the fall of 1868, when he toured the East and the Midwest as the peer of Ward, Nasby, and Billings. He was already surpassing them, and eventually he outlasted them. When he dictated his autobiography in 1906, he reflected on 'the surprising fact that within the compass of these forty years wherein I have been playing professional humorist before the public, I have had for company seventy-eight other American humorists. Each and every one of the seventy-eight rose in my time, became conspicuous and popular, and by and by vanished.' They vanished, he went on to say, confident of his own place in history, 'because they were merely humorists. Humorists of the "mere" sort cannot survive. . . . Humor must not professedly teach and it must not professedly preach, but it must do both if it would live forever. By forever, I mean thirty years.'

Clemens's third venture of early 1867 took him abroad. On 8 June he boarded the sidewheel steamer *Quaker City* and sailed from New York on a five-month tour of Europe and the Middle East. He returned in November a national celebrity as a result of his travel correspondence, and he found waiting for him what he later called 'the *last* link—the conspicuous, the consummating, the victorious link' in the long chain of events that led from Hannibal by way of a special providence to his vocation as a literary person.* This link was a letter from Elisha Bliss, Jr, of Hartford, Connecticut, a publisher of books by subscription. 'I was asked to *write a book*, and I did it, and called it *The Innocents Abroad*.'

'When a subscription book of mine sells sixty thousand, I always think I know whither fifty thousand of them went', he was to say. 'They went to people who don't visit bookstores.' His decision to publish with Bliss implicitly defined his first audiences. The subscription publisher sent out his army of door-to-door agents to solicit orders from small businessmen, tradesmen, professionals, farmers. *The Innocents Abroad*, which sold a hundred thousand copies within two years of its publication in 1869, was to be found in the front parlor on marble-topped tables along with the family Bible, Horace Greeley's *American Conflict*,

---

* 'There ain't no such thing as an accident,' says the garrulous Jim Blaine in *Roughing It*: 'When my Uncle Lem was leaning up agin a scaffolding once, sick, or drunk, or sumthin, an Irishman with a hod full of bricks fell on him out of the third story and broke the old man's back in two places. People said it was an accident. Much accident there was about that. He didn't know what he was there for, but he was there for a good object. If he hadn't been there the Irishman would have been killed. Nobody can ever make me believe anything different from that. Uncle Lem's dog was there. Why didn't the Irishman fall on the dog? Becuz the dog would 'a' seen him a-coming and stood from under. That's the reason the dog warn't app'inted. A dog can't be depended on to carry out a special prov'dence.' (Part II, Chapter 12.)

Opposite *Broadway winter scene*

James Parton's *People's Book of Biography*, and further works of reference, moral philosophy, patriotism, and home doctoring. In such company *The Innocents Abroad* was a surprise which offered almost sinful delight. It was 'an Indian spring in an alkaline literary desert', Bret Harte said.

In *The Innocents Abroad*, his first success, Mark Twain wrote, 'I basked in the happiness of being for once in my life drifting in the tide of a great popular movement.' During the summer of 1867 four or five thousand Americans were leaving for Europe each week, but the *Quaker City* trip, sponsored by Henry Ward Beecher's Plymouth Church and captained by one of Beecher's Sunday-school superintendents, was no routine crossing. It was the original luxury cruise, and the passengers, who were committed to each other's society until they returned to New York in the fall, were, for the most part, prosperous, middle-aged, and godly, having been selected, or at least impressed, by a 'pitiless' Committee on Applications.

Clemens had recognized in the venture an incomparable comic opportunity. He went along as much to observe the sightseers as to see the sights themselves. The *Quaker City* passengers were travel-hungry and culture-hungry, eager to put their home-grown certainties and pieties to the test among the monuments of the Old World and the Holy Land, and Samuel Clemens, through the comic education and disillusioning of his narrator, Mark Twain, was to be their spokesman and their satirist, even their pupil. Without hypocrisy, but with a certain willing suspension of identity, the veteran of Virginia City and San Francisco journalism now submitted himself to the tutelage—in manners, morals, and even in writing—of the *Quaker City* women, in particular a matronly Cleveland bluestocking, Mary Mason Fairbanks. For thirty-two subsequent years Clemens addressed her as 'Mother' and called himself her 'Cub' and her 'Reformed Prodigal'. Gentility, high sentiment, polish, piety, and decorum, along with an aversion to 'slang', 'vulgarity', and irreverence, were her literary and life values, just as they were the values of an entire female reading audience which Mark Twain several times tried to accommodate. One of his contemporaries described this audience as 'the iron Madonna who strangles in her fond embrace the American novelist'.

Under Mrs Fairbanks's tutelage he began to curb his natural bent for burlesque and for what was, by her standards, a certain brutality and

Opposite *Twilight, San Giorgio Maggiore, Venice by Claude Monet, 1908. 'Towers and domes and steeples drowsing in a golden mist of sunset.'* The Innocents Abroad

coarseness that had run through his work from the very beginning.
(She could have cited, among other examples: 'They all jumped on him
at once like a batch of Irish on a sick nigger'; and, 'His breath smells
like a graveyard after an earthquake.') He was also beginning to expand
his notion of the humorist's range and function.

Mary Mason Fairbanks. 'As long-suffering, withal, as a natural mother.'
Letter to his family, 1868

Regarding the *Quaker City* passengers as a class, Clemens admired
their skepticism, their 'roving, independent, free and easy character',
their refusal to be awed by tradition and history. 'Christopher Columbo
—pleasant name,' says one of Mark Twain's pilgrims to an appalled
guide in Genoa, 'is—is he dead?' The same raucous and derisive humor
runs through the narrator's comments on foreigners in general ('They
spell it *Vinci* and pronounce it *Vinchy*; foreigners always spell better
than they pronounce') and on the European present as well as the
European past. Sometimes this humor yields to rage, disgust, and a
peculiar kind of democratic scorn. The citizens of Torre Annunziata,
Clemens reported to the *Alta California* in August 1867,

crowd you—infest you—swarm about you, and sweat and stink, and lie, and
look sneaking, and mean, and obsequious—the concentrated essence of the
soulless, dust-licking scum of the earth the lower classes of the whole nation
are! There is no office too degrading or disgusting for them to perform, for
money. I have had no chance to find out anything about the upper classes by
my own observation, but from what I hear said about them I judge that what
they lack in one or two of the vile traits the *canaille* have, they make up in
one or two others that are infinitely meaner.

And as for the historic past, as he wrote from Gibraltar:

> The ancients considered the Pillars of Hercules the head of navigation and the end of the world. The information the ancients didn't have, was very voluminous. . . . Even the prophets wrote book after book and epistle after epistle, yet never once hinted at the existence of a great continent on our side of the water, yet they must have known it was there, I should think. They knew beforehand what was going to happen, and surely they ought to have known what already existed. But no, they left the ancient public to believe that the Pillars of Hercules was the head of navigation, and Columbus was the first practical prophet to come out and tell them any better.

Predictably, in this derisive view, the Holy Land turned out to be a shabby landscape of rocks and camel dung, the Jordan just a creek, the Dead Sea a fraud, the Sea of Galilee scarcely different from an ordinary city reservoir. Moses took forty years to lead the children of Israel from Egypt to the Promised Land; the overland stage could have done it in thirty-six hours. His book had a purpose, Mark Twain declared in his Preface, 'which is, to suggest to the reader how *he* would be likely to see Europe and the East if he looked at them with his own eyes instead of the eyes of those who traveled in those countries before him'.

Can-can. 'I placed my hands before my face for very shame. But I looked through my fingers.' The Innocents Abroad

But Clemens derided, in Mark Twain as well as in the other pilgrims, a crushing sense of national superiority and assorted qualities of sanctimoniousness, gullibility, parochialism, close-fistedness, and savagery. Travel, he said, broadened some of these 'American Vandals' only in the sense that now they scribbled their names on ruins in foreign lands instead of on privy walls at home. In a bitter mood at the end of the voyage he described the passengers as a congregation of hypocrites, and their months together as 'a funeral excursion without a corpse'. Years later a photograph of one of the passengers provoked the comment, 'It is the way God looks when He has had a successful season', and in acrimonious public statements he described Charles C. Duncan, the captain (or 'head-waiter') of the *Quaker City* as 'a canting hypocrite, filled to the chin with sham godliness, and forever oozing and dripping false piety and pharisaical prayers'.

Holyland tourist in full dress. 'Fantastic mob of green-spectacled Yanks . . . flapping elbows and bobbing umbrellas.' Illustration from The Innocents Abroad

Back from Europe, Clemens spent the fall and winter of 1867–8 in Washington, part of the time as disgruntled and rebellious secretary to Senator William M. Stewart of Nevada. When the proprietors of the *Alta California* suddenly challenged his rights in the *Quaker City* correspondence, he rushed back to San Francisco to settle with them and then to settle down to the writing of *The Innocents Abroad*. Bret Harte helped him to polish and trim his manuscript, to squeeze the wind and the water out of the original correspondence. 'Harte read all the MS. of the "Innocents" and told me what passages, paragraphs, and *chapters* to leave out—and I followed orders strictly', Clemens wrote in 1870, by which time the two seemed pitted against each other in their ordeals by success. 'It was a kind thing for Harte to do, and I think I appreciated it.' But it was Clemens's development of the character of Mark Twain, the narrator, that gave the book its main structural principle and its unique voice; as Harte said when he came to review the book, 'The irascible pilgrim, "Mark Twain," is a very eccentric creation of Mr. Clemens.'

Mark Twain in turn liberated Samuel Clemens to test out his powers and also to begin to discover his usable past and to translate it into literature. As an account of travel, education, adventure, and the encounter of cultures, *The Innocents Abroad* exists vividly in the narrator's present. But more and more insistently as he goes along, the narrator measures not his distance from the past but his closeness, and he looks back to what he calls 'that canonized epoch' of Hannibal and the river. A stone figure in Milan reminds him of the dead man in Judge Clemens's office. When he sees the Pyramid of Cheops he thinks of 'Holliday's Hill, in our town, to me the noblest work of God'. The Sphinx itself comes to stand for this process of recovery of the past: 'It was the type of an attribute of man—of a faculty of heart and brain. It was Memory—Retrospection.'

'I sit here at home in San Francisco,' Clemens wrote at the end of *The Innocents Abroad*, having voyaged 'drearily over accumulating reams of paper.' Home was the Occidental Hotel, breakfast cocktails at the Cliff House, champagne dinners, days and evenings with Harte and his group, all the Bohemian pleasures and freedoms of the 'life of don't-care-a-damn' that he gave up when he became established in the East. He delivered a farewell lecture at the beginning of July 1868 and sailed for New York. He never in all his life went back to San Francisco or California, and not until almost thirty years later, when he was lecturing his way out of bankruptcy, did he even face west again across the Pacific.

'I saw her first in the form of an ivory miniature in her brother Charley's stateroom in the steamer *Quaker City*, in the Bay of Smyrna, in the summer of 1867, when she was in her twenty-second year.' Samuel Clemens met Olivia Langdon in the flesh at Christmas 1867, and they went together to hear Charles Dickens read at Steinway Hall in New York. The circumstances of this evening that Clemens spent with his future wife were fitting. This was the farewell reading in America of a hero of the same avid, mass audience which would soon elevate to a comparable

Left *Steinway Hall, 109–111 East 14th Street, New York.* Above right *'The real fortune of my life.' Olivia Langdon: 'I saw her first in the form of an ivory minia-ture . . . in the summer of 1867, when she was in her twenty-second year.'* Auto-biography. Below right *Charles Dickens by Spy, 1870. 'When Charles Dickens sleeps in this room next week it will be a gratification to him to know that I have slept in it also.' Letter to family, 1867*

eminence the newcomer Mark Twain, also a brilliant public performer and a consummate actor. Despite his awe of Dickens, 'this puissant god', Clemens was disappointed. The readings from *David Copperfield* struck him as monotonous, the pathos as merely verbal—'glittering frost work with no heart'. So he reported to his California paper.

He also reported, 'I am proud to observe that there was a beautiful young lady with me—a highly respectable young white woman.' In an account which he dictated nearly forty years later, he fitted that evening with Livy into a characteristic knot of associations and motives for, at the height of his Hartford years with Livy, love, happiness, literary fame, and money were convertible currency. Charles Dickens made two hundred thousand dollars from his readings in America that season, but that single evening with Livy 'made the fortune of my life—not in dollars, I am not thinking of dollars; it made the real fortune of my life in that it made the happiness of my life'. The following August, having delivered the manuscript of *The Innocents Abroad* to his publisher, Clemens presented himself at the gate of the Langdons' baronial establishment on Main Street in Elmira, New York.

Coal, iron, and an intimate rate alliance with the Delaware, Lackawanna, and Western Railway had made Jervis Langdon and his family rich. They were provincial gentry, former abolitionists, present supporters of the freedmen and Frederick Douglass, mainstays of the Elmira community and of Elmira's First Congregational Church, whose pastor was Henry Ward Beecher's brother Thomas. It apparently did not occur to the Langdons that their rough and alien house guest could be a possible suitor for their daughter Livy. She had led a more sheltered life than most and was more delicate. At sixteen, after falling on the ice, she had suffered an obscure disabling injury to her spine; the damage seems to have been largely hysterical in nature, for after two years in a darkened room she had been cured by an itinerant mind healer who said to her, 'Now we will walk a few steps, my child', and she did. During her invalidism she had been educated by a tutor and by the Reverend Mr Beecher, who together neglected her spelling and her composition but instilled a conventional Christianity and a powerful, if untested, sense of right and wrong.

She had the 'heart-free laugh of a girl', Clemens said, and remembering the domestic austerities of his early life, he was quick to sense in her an immense capacity for giving. She 'poured out her prodigal affections in kisses and caresses,' he said, 'and in a vocabulary of endearments whose profusion was always an astonishment to me'. She was also gentle, calm, refined, spiritual (myopia intensified her look of musing intensity), and undeniably beautiful. In almost everyone who knew her and left a record of his impression she seems to have inspired something close to adulation.

Clemens was in love; after less than two weeks in the Langdon house he proposed to her, and she said no. 'I do not regret that I have loved you, still love you, and shall always love you', he wrote in the first of nearly two hundred letters she was to receive from him before their marriage in February 1870. 'I believe in you even as I believe in the Saviour', he was to say a little later, explaining, in an avowal of romantic paganism that was the true clue to his 'conversion', that his faith was 'as simple and unquestioning as the faith of a devotee in the idol he worships'. 'Perhaps', he was to say more than thirty years later, 'it was nearly like a subject's feeling for his sovereign—a something which he does not have to reason out, or study about, but which comes natural.' He had invested her with a power she scarcely suspected, so that when she spoke the word 'disapprove', it had the force, for him, of another person's 'damn'.

Livy disapproved of drinking, smoking, Western manners, and even humorists, and he courted her by offering, in all sincerity, to make over his character and his habits to meet her desires. For a while he came close to religious orthodoxy, prayed, went to church, wrote a purple meditation on the Nativity, showed signs of intending to write a life of Christ, and even ended a love letter to Livy with, 'Goodbye—with a kiss of reverent honor and another of deathless affection—and—Hebrews, XIII, 20, 21.'

But such piety and plasticity scarcely outlasted his courtship. In the larger pattern of their life together Livy's power over him was chiefly that of an instructed proxy for whose sake he made the concessions he had been willing to make in the first place. 'The idol is the measure of the worshipper,' said James Russell Lowell; in choosing Livy as his idol Clemens chose his own willed transformations.

Olivia Langdon

All the while, as a way of dealing with inevitably conflictive feelings about these transformations, he made wry jokes and complaints the effect of which was to put blame on Livy by portraying him as blissfully henpecked, a man entirely under his wife's thumb, a suppressed writer. 'His wife not only edited his works but edited him,' said Van Wyck

Brooks, who may have taken these public statements too much at face value. As nearly every major decision of Mark Twain's life—literary and otherwise—seems to demonstrate, Livy reigned rather than ruled and was less his censor than his muse.

He was even to withdraw the concessions he made while he was courting Livy. He took the pledge then, for example, but within a few years Livy was drinking ale as a tonic and before going to bed, while he drank medicinal cocktails of Scotch and bitters before breakfast, hot whiskies at night, and a variety of beverages in between. Her declared opposition to smoking had comparable results—he was to say much later that the only 'rules' he observed in this matter were 'never to smoke more than one cigar at a time'. He did not become a Christian as he had promised to do, but instead became a foe of institutional and doctrinal Christianity, while Livy's faith, secure and unquestioned until her marriage, was eroded to a point where, at the end of her life, it no longer offered her spiritual shelter and refuge. He blamed himself for this— 'Almost the only crime of my life which causes me bitterness now', he said in 1905.

On tour, Clemens returned to Elmira in November 1868 and a six-day siege, during which Livy came to hear him lecture. 'She said over and over again that she loved me', he reported. Livy was easier to win than her parents. After recovering from their first grief and shock at learning how things stood, they began an investigation of his history, which 'came within an ace of breaking off my marriage'. The questions the Langdons asked about his former standard of conduct and habitual life implied inevitable answers: from sources in San Francisco, Livy's parents began to hear that her suitor was a 'humbug' who 'has talent ... but will make a trivial use of it' and probably 'would fill a drunkard's grave'. In the end Jervis Langdon, impressed by Clemens's absolute refusal to deny his past and so 'live backwards', gave his assent.

The formal engagement announced on 4 February 1869, began a year of miracles during which it seemed that all things were possible. As a base for the steady life he vowed to live henceforth, Clemens, with the aid of a substantial loan from Langdon, bought a one-third interest in the *Express*, a daily paper located in Buffalo and therefore well within the sphere of the family's business interests. In July the publication of *The Innocents Abroad* began to bring him fame and money to a degree he would not have dared predict, more lecturing and writing invitations than he could possibly fill, and a national reputation through the popular press. But there was recognition, too, from quarters where subscription books generally found little favor. In December the *Atlantic Monthly* carried a prophetic review by its young assistant editor, William Dean Howells, soon to become Clemens's intimate friend, literary adviser, and literary hero. ('You are really my only author,' he told Howells some years later; 'I wouldn't give a damn for the rest.') 'There is an amount of pure human nature in the book that rarely gets into literature', Howells said in his review—

> Under his *nom de plume* of Mark Twain, Mr. Clemens is well known to the very large world of newspaper readers; and this book ought to secure him something better than the uncertain standing of a popular favorite. It is no business of ours to fix his rank among the humorists California has given us, but we think he is, in an entirely different way from all the others, quite worthy of the company of the best.

Finally, on 2 February 1870, after a triumphant lecture tour which began in Pittsburgh with an oyster supper and ended, after nearly sixty performances, in Jamestown, New York, Clemens and Livy were married in Elmira. The wedding party traveled by private railroad car to Buffalo, where a breathtaking and gaudy surprise, the gift of Jervis Langdon, awaited the bridegroom: an elegantly furnished three-story mansion on a fashionable street. A cook, coachman, and housemaid greeted him; in the stable behind the house were horse and carriage. Wealth and love had become synonymous. 'We are as happy in our Aladdin's palace', Clemens soon said, 'as if we were roosting in the closing chapters of a popular novel.'

A few days after the wedding Clemens made some crucial associations between his new happiness and his materials as a writer. 'The fountains of my great deep are broken up', he wrote to an old Hannibal friend,

> and I have rained reminiscences for four and twenty hours. The old life has swept before me like a panorama; the old days have trooped by in their old glory again; the old faces have looked out of the mists of the past; old foot-steps have sounded in my listening ears; old hands have clasped mine, and songs I loved ages and ages ago have come wailing down the centuries. Heavens what eternities have swung their hoary cycles about us since those days were new!—Since we tore down Dick Hardy's stable; since you had the

Opposite Above *Buffalo. Lithograph by D. Appleton and Co., 1873.* Below left *The American Humorists: Petroleum V. Nasby, Mark Twain, Josh Billings. On tour, November 1869.* Below centre *Jervis Langdon's wedding present to his son-in-law: 472 Delaware Avenue, Buffalo.* Below right *Mark Twain's son, Langdon Clemens, born 1870, died 1872*

measles and I went to your house purposely to catch them; since Henry
Beebe kept that envied slaughter-house, and Joe Craig sold him cats to
kill in it; since old General Gaines used to say, 'Whoop! Bow your neck and
spread!'; since Jimmy Finn was town drunkard and we stole his dinner
while he slept in the vat and fed it to the hogs in order to keep them still till
we could mount them and have a ride. . . .

This flooding of memory goes on for about seven hundred words and ends
with a sudden transition to the transfigured present.

> For behold I have at this moment the only sweetheart I ever *loved*, and bless
> her old heart she is lying asleep upstairs in a bed that I sleep in every night,
> and for four whole days she has been *Mrs. Samuel L. Clemens!*

It was to be more than a year, however, before Mark Twain, the victim
of misjudgment and malign harassments of various sorts, found himself
as a writer once again—and not in Buffalo but in Hartford. In August
1870, his father-in-law died, and Livy had a nervous collapse. In September
a friend died of typhus in Clemens's own bed and bedroom. In October,
Livy had a near-miscarriage and was confined to the library downstairs;
in November she gave birth to a premature, frail, and sickly boy,
Langdon (who died at nineteen months); and in the spring she came down
with typhoid fever. By this time Clemens was 'simply half-crazy' with
fatigue and despair—'And I wish I was the other half.' He had lost all
interest in his newspaper and was scarcely in a mood to write the ten
pages of humor each month that a New York magazine, *The Galaxy*, had
contracted for. In July, full of confidence and enthusiasm, he had begun
to 'do up Nevada and Cal.' in *Roughing It*; by November he was in a
mood of utter defeat about the new book—'*I am sitting still with idle
hands*', he told Orion.

In December he wrote a hoax review of *The Innocents Abroad* for *The
Galaxy*. Pretending to be a stubbornly and literal-minded English critic,
he took Mark Twain to task for his 'insolence, presumption, mendacity
and ignorance'. Compounding the implicit self-hatred, the hoax back-
fired: despite his outraged protests and challenges the review was
accepted as genuine, and the joke was on him. And all the while, at a
time when he had hit bottom and fancied that he was hearing 'a popular
author's death rattle', the star of Bret Harte rose and blazed in the sky.
With the publication of a poem popularly called 'The Heathen Chinee'
and of his collection of stories, *The Luck of Roaring Camp*, Harte became
'the most celebrated man in America today,' Clemens said in March 1871,
'the man whose name is on every single tongue from one end of the
continent to the other'. (When Harte traveled east across the continent

in that year, Clemens recalled much later, 'one might have supposed he was the Viceroy of India on a progress, or Halley's comet come again after seventy-five years of lamented absence'.) As a result of a misunderstanding involving the reviewing of *The Innocents Abroad*, the relationship of Clemens and Bret Harte had entered one of its cyclic periods of cold enmity. It was impossible for Clemens not to believe that Bret Harte's rise meant his own eclipse.

What Clemens associated with Buffalo now was not the night he had entered his gaslit fairyland on Delaware Avenue but instead months of illness, death, drudgery, and defeat. In March 1871 he put up for sale the Buffalo house and his share in the *Express*, two ties to a way of life which, he had painfully learned, was Jervis Langdon's, not his own. He took Livy to Quarry Farm, his sister-in-law's country place near Elmira, and soon, with the encouragement of a visit from Joe Goodman, who had hired him for the *Enterprise*, he was back at work on *Roughing It*, writing with increasing joy, confidence, and 'red-hot interest'. It was going to be a 'bully book', a 'starchy book', he said. Chapter 8, his account of the Pony Express rider was 'by all odds the finest piece of writing I ever did', he told Elisha Bliss. And along with this complete swing in mood came evidence that his reputation had survived its crisis; he was flooded with offers for books and almanacs, articles and lectures. 'The reaction is beginning and my stock is looking up.' In October, finally committed to a career as full-time writer, restored in strength and faith by his summer of work on *Roughing It*, he moved to Hartford and entered the most productive period of his life.

THE
CITY HALL,
PHILADELPHIA.

Chapter Four

The Gilded Age
1871–9

'I never saw any place where morality and huckleberries flourished as they do here', Clemens wrote after a visit to his publisher in Hartford. He was seeing huckleberries for the first time. Within a few years, the huckleberry, a Hartford association (and then also a slang term for a person of no consequence) fused with his recollection of Jimmy Finn, Hannibal's town drunk, and became a talisman for recovering the past. At the same time, following the other current of his life, Mark Twain moved forward from Hartford into the incentives and rewards of what he celebrated as 'our great Century'.

Hartford, the most prosperous of American cities in the 1870s, stood midway in values as well as distance between New York's scrambling commerce and Boston's official culture. Boston never accepted Mark Twain without strains and abrasions on both sides. 'I cannot say why Clemens seemed not to hit the favor of our community of scribes and scholars, as Bret Harte had done,' Howells wrote of his friend's uneasy relationship with Boston and Cambridge, 'but it is certain that he did not, and I had better say so.' But Nook Farm, a suburban grove which nested in Hartford's larger structure and regarded itself as a dynamic aristocracy open to talent and ideas, welcomed Mark Twain among its élite. He shared the community's dedication to invested capital, large houses, lavish hospitality, and a distinctive mixture of informality and decorum, grandeur and simplicity. His closest friend in Hartford was to be a clergyman, the Reverend Joseph H. Twichell, pastor of the Asylum Hill Congregational Church, an opulent structure renamed by Mark

Opposite *One expression of the spirit of the Gilded Age: the Philadelphia City Hall carried gimcrackery about as far (and as high) as it could go*

Twain, in honor of the flock's considerable stake in the economy of the Gilded Age, 'The Church of the Holy Speculators'.

Clemens's Nook Farm neighbors, Harriet Beecher Stowe and Charles Dudley Warner, were professional writers who could command a comfortable living from their work. They welcomed him all the more warmly because he showed promise of becoming the most productive and professional author of them all. *Roughing It*, published in February 1872, was not the success he had anticipated; still, it proved to him that *The Innocents Abroad* had been no fluke. He told Livy that the general verdict was that the new book was 'much better written', and after Howells's approving review appeared in the *Atlantic* he said, 'I am as uplifted and reassured by it as a mother who has given birth to a white baby when she was awfully afraid it was going to be a mulatto.' The following year he published a novel, *The Gilded Age*, written in collaboration with Warner. The panic of 1873 hurt the sales of the book, but his own loose dramatization as a stage vehicle for the comic actor John T. Raymond, in the part of Colonel Sellers, became one of the more popular plays of the 1870s; in three years, Clemens figured, the book and the play together earned for him about a hundred thousand dollars. In 1875 he published a collection, *Sketches, New and Old*, and, as a regular contributor to the *Atlantic*, a series of seven articles on piloting, which later became the first half of *Life on the Mississippi*. In 1876 he published *The Adventures of Tom Sawyer* and began the long, troubled composition of *Huckleberry Finn*.

The exuberant variety of Mark Twain's energies and interests mirrored his country and his times. He was a star lecturer in England as well as America; novelist; short-story writer; social historian; dramatist; magazine journalist; incomparable raconteur and enthusiastic billiard player; lavish host; devoted family man; the inventor of 'Mark Twain's Self-Pasting Scrapbook' and other patentable devices, including an 'Improvement in Adjustable and Detachable Straps for Garments' and a board game played with pegs and pins; investor in a domestic still for desalinating water, an improved steam generator for tugboats, and some 'new kind of steam pulley' (ventures which promised him 'millions' but yielded nothing). Industrializing his own profession, he sent a friend to the South African diamond fields to gather material for a new book by Mark Twain which was certain to be 'brimful of fame and fortune'; the project turned out to be another kind of steam pulley. He

Opposite *Hornellsville, New York. Lithograph by Currier and Ives. 'The drive and push and rush and struggle of the raging, tearing, booming nineteenth century.'* Speeches

TO THE GRAND ARMY OF THE REPUBLIC
This print of
OUR OLD COMMANDER
GENERAL U. S. GRANT
is Respectfully dedicated

was even director of an accident-insurance company, and in a hilarious and gruesome speech later issued as an advertising pamphlet he praised what was, along with his own work and the flow of small arms from the Colt factory, this most distinctive of Hartford's contributions to the national happiness:

> I have seen an entire family lifted out of poverty and into affluence by the simple boon of a broken leg. I have had people come to me on crutches, with tears in their eyes, to bless this beneficent institution. In all my experience of life, I have seen nothing so seraphic as the look that comes into a freshly mutilated man's face when he feels in his vest pocket with his remaining hand and finds his accident ticket all right.

In all, he was well on his way to achieving the eminence of a national and even international institution. 'You Americans have Mark Twain and *Harper's* Magazine', an English guide said to a group of tourists in 1882. The following year, Thomas Hardy said at a London dinner party, 'Why don't people understand that Mark Twain is not merely a great humorist? He is a remarkable fellow in a very different way', and he went on to praise *Life on the Mississippi*, a book also admired by Kaiser Wilhelm II of Germany. In 1895 Clemens was to note that people in India knew only three things about America—'George Washington, Mark Twain, and the Chicago Fair.'

Such celebrity fed upon and reproduced itself in an endless cycle of newspaper stories and anecdotes, witticisms genuine or attributed, requests for interviews, autographs, pictures, comments, and advice. Samuel Clemens, who jealously guarded his own and his family's privacy but was also a genius at generating publicity, had created Mark Twain, a public figure recognizable on almost any street in America by his rolling gait, his unruly mustache and cascade of graying curls, his vivid winter costumes of sealskin coat and fur hat. Even a walk from Hartford to Boston which he undertook in 1874 and never finished—he gave up after thirty-five miles and went the rest of the way by train— became, under his shrewd management, a public event, a comic pilgrimage with satiric overtones.* Sometimes he regretted the celebrity

---

* The Boston 'walk', which ended with a scalloped-oyster feast at Howells's house in Cambridge, recalled Charles Dickens's 'Great International Walking Match' of 1868. Dickens walked competitively from Boston to Newton Center and back and then gave a fancy literary dinner at the Parker House.

Opposite General U.S. Grant. Lithograph by Currier and Ives. 'You have written a book, too,' Mark Twain teased Grant, 'and when it is published you can hold up your head and let on to be a person of consequence.'

The South African diamond fields, subject for a book (unwritten) which promised to 'sweep the world like a besom of destruction'.

he had achieved and became snappish and resentful or tried to hide under incognitos, registering at hotels as Samuel Langhorne, C. L. Samuel, J. P. Smith, or J. P. Jones.

When Mark Twain arrived in Hartford in October 1871 he was in moderate financial difficulties. Within three years, and drawing on Livy's inheritance, he moved his family from a rented house to a mansion he built on a five-acre tract of land on Farmington Avenue. The house was an eye-catching complex of turrets, polychrome brick, balconies, verandas, and embrasures, which enclosed nineteen principal rooms and a variety of wonders—a guest room shaped like a pilothouse, a schoolroom where the children were tutored by Livy and a governess, a glassed-in conservatory where, through the coldest of New England winters, a fountain played amidst calla lilies and flowering vines. This stately mansion, as Howells called it, had cost its owner about one hundred and twenty-five thousand dollars to begin with (he was to go on to extensive renovations and enlargements in 1881) and committed him to a style of living and earning more like that of a robber baron than that of a writer; from time to time the expense of being possessed by this establishment would drive the Clemenses off to Europe for a period of thrift and retrenchment. At home, he and Livy, with the aid of a nursemaid, housemaid, laundress, cook, butler, and coachman, dispensed hospitality to such a steady stream of neighbors, visitors, and celebrities that she was often prostrated with fatigue, while the only prolonged work he was able to do was generally done during the summers, at Quarry Farm—the Hartford house, for all its spaciousness, never provided a satisfactory place for him to write in.

Number 351 Farmington Avenue—part steamboat, part medieval stronghold, part cuckoo clock, and in all respects the opposite extreme from the 'birdhouse' on Hill Street in Hannibal—was Nook Farm's gaudiest landmark and an American success story. In Veblen's phrase about the architecture of the robber barons, it was 'a sort of visible bank balance'. The Word had been made bricks and mortar, and Mark Twain dwelt among them, enjoying an almost magical prosperity which, he told Howells and Thomas Bailey Aldrich, two dazzled authors from frugal Boston, derived chiefly from 'the satisfying, the surfeiting nature

Opposite *In his sealskin winter outfit: a public figure recognizable on almost any street in America.* Other pictures, top to bottom *Prospect Street, Hartford. Library and Conservatory, 351 Farmington Avenue. Nook Farm neighbor: Charles Dudley Warner's house. Quarry Farm, overlooking Elmira: summering place for the Clemens family*

of subscription publishing'. 'Anything but subscription publishing', he said, 'is printing for private circulation.'

For Mark Twain during the 1870s Nook Farm was a sheltering enclave walled off from a demoralized nation and 'an era of incredible rottenness'. He put the bitter credo of that era into the mouth of one of its representative men, 'Boss' Tweed of Tammany Hall:

> What is the chief end of man?—to get rich. In what way?—dishonestly if we can; honestly if we must. Who is God, the one only and true? Money is God. Gold and Greenbacks and Stock—father, son, and the ghost of same—three persons in one; these are the true and only God, mighty and supreme: and William Tweed is his prophet.

Two visits to England merely confirmed his growing disgust with his own country. He had gone over alone, in the fall of 1872, with the plan of writing a satirical travel book. Almost on landing, though, he discovered that he adored the English too much to satirize them and that they, in turn, adored him too much for him to repay them with anything less than love. Back home the occupation of humorist had a shaky status and weak defenses. Such eminences as Dr Josiah Gilbert Holland, the editor and one of the founders of *Scribner's Monthly*, publicly denounced entertainers like Mark Twain as 'jesters and mountebanks', 'triflers', and 'literary buffoons'. But when Clemens, in self-defense, called Holland 'a remorseless intellectual cholera' and a 'perambulating sack of chloroform', he said this privately, in an unpublished manuscript titled in resignation 'An Appeal from One That Is Persecuted'.

But in England Clemens found that *The Innocents Abroad* and *Roughing It*, in pirated as well as authorized editions, had made him the hero of a tremendous vogue for American humor and the American West; even the Poet Laureate, Mr Tennyson, longed to hear him lecture. There was no class division in English taste and adulation so far as Mark Twain was concerned. Every door was open to him, he was applauded everywhere, and the great men of England—intellectuals, writers, politicians—waited upon him; he dined with a Plantagenet, walked arm in arm with the Lord Chancellor. 'I did not know I was a lion', Clemens told Livy, utterly intoxicated by the warmth of his welcome, and in the summer of 1873 he brought her there with him to share his triumph, his pleasure, and the landscape. 'Rural England is too absolutely beautiful to be left out of doors', he exclaimed. 'Ought to be under a glass case.'

England stood for stability, continuity, a serene and unitary culture, government by a dedicated and responsible élite. At home he seemed to see only chicanery and cynicism, a corrupt and demoralized civil

London: The Horse Guards on parade

service, rampant abuses of suffrage and legislative power, judicial frauds like the jury system. 'Low foreheads and heavy faces they all had', he wrote of a murder jury in *The Gilded Age*; 'some had a look of animal cunning, while the most were only stupid'. In the White House, Ulysses Grant, a victor in war but a fool in peace, was mired in scandal. A massive national disgrace had just been exposed in the affairs of the Crédit Mobilier, and it seemed at times that, if anyone wanted to buy it, the entire federal government was for sale, and especially Congress. A sample body of 'the smallest minds and the selfishest souls and the cowardliest hearts that God makes', Mark Twain said years later; and at other stages in his life he returned to the theme with savage delight—'It could probably be shown by facts and figures that there is no distinctly native American criminal class except Congress', and 'I think I can say, and say with pride, that we have some legislators that bring higher prices than any in the world.'

Closer to Nook Farm, and dividing it against itself, was the scandal of Mrs Stowe's famous brother, Henry Ward Beecher, now implicated in an adulterous relationship with a parishioner. The shepherd had turned wolf, and the entire protracted scandal—'the Beecher horror', Lowell called it—became for Mark Twain yet another evidence of 'incredible rottenness'. 'This nation is not reflected in Charles Sumner,' he told Orion, 'but in Henry Ward Beecher, Benjamin Butler, Whitelaw Reid, William M. Tweed. *Politics* are not going to cure moral ulcers like these, nor the decaying body they fester upon.' A dinner guest at Farmington Avenue in 1875 noted, 'He is overwhelmed with shame and confusion and wishes he were not an American.' The guest was scarcely more dismayed than Mary Fairbanks's daughter, to whom he declared his loathing for 'all shades and forms of republican government'. He would only be doing his duty, he said, if he succeeded in winning her generation over 'to an honest and saving loathing for universal suffrage'.

By the end of the decade Mark Twain's 'Anglomania' (as Howells called it) and his antirepublicanism would subside and begin to yield to their opposites: he became, in time, a symbolic American and a symbolic democrat. Yet during the early 1870s, instead of a satire on the English, he wrote *The Gilded Age*, a satirical and topical book about democracy gone off the tracks. It echoes the sounds of its times—the rustle of greenbacks and the hiss of steam, the clang of railroad iron and the boom of blasting charges, the quiet talk of men in committee rooms and bankers' offices. Its raw materials are glittering schemes and blighted hopes, bribery, hypocrisy, blackmail, murder, and mob violence. Its most vivid and brilliant character, Colonel Beriah Sellers, is, above all, the Promoter, that distinctive profession of the era. 'I've got the biggest scheme on earth, and I'll take you in; I'll take in every friend I've got that's ever stood by me, for there's enough for all, and to spare.' This, along with his visionary cry of 'There's millions in it', echoed through Mark Twain's entire life, from the time of the Tennessee land on through his involvement in the Paige typesetter and other chimeras. At the end of *The Gilded Age* even the naïvest of its characters succumbs to a sense of futility—'The country is a fool.'

Joe Goodman was appalled when he read *The Prince and the Pauper*, a romance set in sixteenth-century England. 'What could have sent you groping among the driftwood of the Deluge for a topic,' he asked, 'when you would have been so much more at home in the wash of today?' One answer may have been that Mark Twain felt that he could deal with 'the wash of today' only as a satirist and moralist who could barely keep his

Opposite *Bret Harte by* Spy. *'I think his heart was merely a pump and had no other function.'* Autobiography. Overleaf *351 Farmington Avenue, Hartford, completed in 1874. 'Mr Clemens seems to glory in his sense of possession,' his wife said.*

anger and disgust in check. While Howells, Aldrich, Warner, and Harriet Beecher Stowe turned to their early years for subjects and helped create what turned into a cult of childhood, Mark Twain, to a greater extent than any of them, and for a longer time, became an expatriate from the Gilded Age his imagination went home instead to Hannibal and the river.

He sighted and approached his central materials in a way which was casual, susceptible to accident and outside influence, but which most of the time vindicated his almost religious faith in the springs of his creativity. 'When the tank runs dry', he learned during the summer of 1874 as he worked on *Tom Sawyer*, 'you've only got to leave it alone and it will fill up again in time.' He once described *Tom Sawyer* as simply 'a hymn, put into prose form to give it a worldly air'. But the book he outlined on the first page of his manuscript dealt with disillusionment, not celebration:

> 1. Boyhood & youth; 2 y[outh] & early manh[ood]; 3 the Battle of Life in many lands; 4 (age 37 to [40?],) return & meet grown babies & toothless old drivelers who were the grandees of his boyhood. The Adored unknown a [illegible] faded old maid & full of rasping, puritanical vinegar piety.

But soon after, this somber précis was followed by an unlocking of memory of the sort he had experienced a few days after his wedding, and he began to translate Hannibal into St Petersburg.

Word by word, sentence by sentence, Mark Twain was a deliberate craftsman, and his ear for the one and only right word, for the rhythms of speech and the shadings of dialect, was unsurpassed. But his planning of fiction on any larger scale than an anecdote or an episode tended to be inspirational, intuitive, indecisive—sometimes it broke down altogether and his work came to a full stop (for years, as with *Huckleberry Finn*). In September 1874 his tank ran dry, he put *Tom Sawyer* aside, and he turned to writing his series about piloting, another approach to the past. The first sentence of his first article began with the invocation that hardly ever failed him: 'When I was a boy. . . .'

It was only by the summer of 1875, when Mark Twain finally finished *Tom Sawyer*, that he decided not to let his story and his hero 'drift into manhood'. Purifying the past of the present, he saved as subjects for his autobiography 'the Battle of Life in many lands' and the disenchantment summed up by the 'faded old maid'. 'Boyhood and youth' were the prime subjects of his fiction. And it was only after consulting Howells and Livy that Mark Twain decided that *Tom Sawyer* was a book for boys

Opposite *The Conservatory, 351 Farmington Avenue. Like other 'greeneries' at Nook Farm it followed Harriet Beecher Stowe's designs.*

instead of grownups and that it should be published that way, 'pure and simple'.

'Altogether the best boy's story I ever read', Howells told him. 'It will be an immense success.' The prediction was eventually correct, but in the short run, by Mark Twain's standards, *Tom Sawyer* was a failure when Bliss published it at the end of 1876. Far from being an early best seller, it sold only about twenty-four thousand copies during its first year, and meanwhile a new book, which Mark Twain thought of as

Above left *Joseph Hopkins Twichell, pastor of 'the Church of the Holy Specu-lators'.* Below left *William Dean Howells. 'You are really my only author,'* Mark Twain said. *'I wouldn't give a damn for the rest.'* Above right *The Reverend Henry Ward Beecher, spellbinder, leader of his flock, 'moral ulcer'.* Below right *Elisha Bliss, Jr, president of the American Publishing Company. 'He has been dead a quarter of a century now . . . and if I could send him a fan I would.'* Autobiography. Opposite page *Playbill for Mark Twain's dramatization of* The Gilded Age

'Huck Finn's Autobiography', had fought him to a complete standstill. He reported its progress to Howells in August 1876:

Began another boys' book—more to be at work than anything else. I have written 400 pages of it—therefore it is very nearly half done. . . . I like it only

VARIETIES THEATRE

MR. CHARLES POPE...............MANAGER

"THERE'S MILLIONS IN IT."

MONDAY, JANUARY 22,

And EVERY EVENING UNTIL FURTHER NOTICE,
THE RENOWNED ARTIST

MR. JOHN T.

RAYMOND

IN HIS MASTERLY PERSONATION OF

COLONEL

Realistic New Scenery by Dressel.

THE HIT OF THE TIMES.

MULBERRY SELLERS

In the famous new American Five Act Drama of that name, by MARK TWAIN, the Greatest of American Characterizations.

COL. GEORGE SELBY, a Confederate	J. P. RUTLEDGE
SI HAWKINS	RUSSELL SOGGS
CLAY HAWKINS, adopted son of Si	C. A. STEDMAN
UNCLE DANIEL, an Old Negro	E. MABBLE
DISTRICT ATTORNEY	J. W. HAGUE
LAFAYETTE HAWKINS, son of Si Hawkins	W. H. WALLACE
JUDGE OF THE COURT	J. DAVIDSON
DUFFER, Counsel for the Defence	H. B. BRADLEY
CLERK OF THE COURT	R. J. BROWNE
JOHN PATTERSON	A. TORRIANNI
FOREMAN OF THE JURY	D. LOGAN
LITTLE LAFAYETTE, (Act 1) aged 12	
LITTLE EMILY, (Act 1) aged 8	ROSA RAND
LAURA HAWKINS, adopted daughter of Mrs. Hawkins	FANNIE LEE
EMILY HAWKINS, daughter of Mrs. Si	MRS NELLIE TAYLOR
MRS. SI HAWKINS	MISS EMMA SANDERSON
MRS. COL. SELLERS	

Act 1—Explosion of the Amaranth.
Act 2—The Napoleon Lots.
Act 3- Sellers' Eye-Water—Expiation.
Act 5—The Trial—Sellers as a Witness.

RAYMOND MATINEE SATURDAY

In elaborate preparation, and soon to be produced—

SAMSON !

Made famous by SALVINI, in which **Mr. CHARLES POPE** will appear.

PICAYUNE STEAM JOB PRINT, 66 CAMP STREET.

tolerably well, as far as I have got, and may possibly pigeonhole it or burn the MS when it is done.

But the tank went dry again and was slow in filling up. He did not burn his manuscript, but he did pigeonhole it, worked on it in 1879 or 1880, put it aside once more, and in 1884, eight years and seven books after he began it, Mark Twain finally finished *Huckleberry Finn.* He had broken off in 1876 baffled by a problem of plot and character motivation and also uncertain as yet just how deeply, searingly, courageously he was going to deal with the profound issues of his story—freedom, the collision within Huck of 'a sound heart' (his natural, better impulses) and 'a deformed conscience' (the voice of custom, education, the community), the unacknowledgable rift between morality and social norms. At the point where Mark Twain broke off in 1876 Huck and the runaway slave Jim, both of them criminals by the code of a slaveholding society, have passed Cairo, Illinois, the last free-soil outpost, and are headed deeper South. A Mississippi steamboat, image of avenging society, pounds down upon the fugitives and destroys their raft, a fragile island of freedom between two hostile shores of society.

Aunt Polly Beguiled. Illustration from The Adventures of Tom Sawyer

'Yes, one of the brightest gems in the New England weather is the dazzling uncertainty of it', Mark Twain said at a banquet in New York City at the end of 1876: 'There is only one thing certain about it: you are certain there is going to be plenty of it—a perfect grand review; but you can never tell which end of the procession is going to move first.'

Uncertainty seemed to be governing his own work and his traffic with the great public he depended upon. *Tom Sawyer* was a 'failure', and *Huckleberry Finn* was at a standstill. During 1877 his most successful book, ironically, was his self-pasting scrapbook, and this had no real writing in it at all. In the summer he witnessed the failure of *Ah Sin*, a play he had written at Nook Farm with Bret Harte during a brief, and this time final, period of cordiality. On opening night in New York at Augustin Daly's Fifth Avenue Theater Clemens spoke ruefully of Daly's attempts as producer and director to rescue from disaster this dismaying comedy written partly in pidgin English and wholly on the assumption that two humorists were funnier than one—'I never saw a play that was so much improved by being cut down; and I believe it would have been one of the very best plays in the world if his strength had held out so that he could cut out the whole of it.'

In November he started making notes for his Tudor romance, *The Prince and the Pauper*. He planned to publish it anonymously, 'such grave and stately work being considered by the world to be above my proper level'. He was to write *Huckleberry Finn* mostly for his own satisfaction, and by many of the standards of the genteel tradition it was an adversary novel. He undertook *A Tramp Abroad*, his European travel book published in 1880, as an act of commerce. But *The Prince and the Pauper*, published in 1882, was one of Mark Twain's intermittent acts of cultural fealty, a costume drama full of ceremonials and historical information which, at one and the same time, catered to the fashionable taste for monarchical England and asserted the superiority of democratic ideals, all without offending anyone whatsoever.

He was determined that this new book would exhibit him not as a humorist but as a serious practitioner of polite, colorful literature designed to entertain and inform children and the family circle. In recognition of his ideal audience he was to dedicate *The Prince and the Pauper* to Susy and Clara Clemens, 'those good-mannered and agreeable children'. The adjectives scarcely suggest his remembered childhood in Hannibal but they anticipate the kind of praise he received for the book. 'Your masterpiece in fineness', Mary Fairbanks told him; Susy regarded it as 'unquestionably the best book he has ever written'; while in the reviews of the day the words 'pure', 'lovely', 'subdued', 'delicate', 'refined', and 'ennobling' recurred as part of the grateful appreciation of just those qualities in Mark Twain which any conventional romancer —including Mrs Frances Hodgson Burnett, the future author of *Little Lord Fauntleroy*—might be expected to possess: professional polish, descriptive power, neatness of plot construction, and an over-all correctness in manner, incident, and language.

Even while he planned his 'good-mannered and agreeable' romance, however, Mark Twain felt certain opposed stirrings within him that he was not yet prepared to acknowledge, even to himself—a growing commitment to criticism of society, a growing impatience with accepted pieties, patriotic, moral, and cultural. In two important speeches he made late in 1877 he was clearly moving away from benign entertainments toward complex and conflictive comic molds. In October he attended a banquet festivity honoring the visit to Hartford—birthplace of the Colt revolver, the Sharps repeating rifle, and the Gatling gun— of the Ancient and Honorable Artillery Company of Massachusetts, the oldest military organization in the country. After listening to a series of orators wave the bloody shirt and recall the good old days of Bull Run and Gettysburg, he paid tribute to the menu—'If you fight as well as you feed, God protect the enemy'—and then spoke daringly and mockingly of his own Civil War service, on the other side. 'I find myself in a minority here.' He described his brief career as rebel soldier and rational coward who, when the Worcestershire sauce ran out and the mosquitoes and even the horses started biting and the fear and boredom began to mount, did not say, 'War is hell', but instead said, 'To hell with war', and lit out for safety and the Territory. There, as his listeners knew, he had had a pretty good time of it, far from the cannon and the battlefields. 'We were the first men that went into the service in Missouri', he said, and added without apology, 'We were the first that went out of it anywhere.' What was the fighting all about, anyhow? In effect, he had asked that almost forbidden question, and although he had no quarrel with the outcome of the Civil War, he continued to ask that question in an increasingly more probing and conscience-stricken way until finally it had less to do with the conflict of North and South than it did with the martial spirit in general. And as he was later to deduce from America's adventures in Cuba and the Philippines and from the jingo politics of Theodore Roosevelt, the martial spirit was clearly one of the driving forces of his country.

In 'The Private History of a Campaign That Failed', published in 1885, he was to translate his Civil War experience into a dark and ironic reading of the experience of all wars. Sam Clemens and the other Marion Rangers, hiding at night in a corncrib, ambush a horseman whom they believe to be one of General Grant's scouts:

The man was not in uniform and was not armed. He was a stranger in the country, that was all we ever found out about him. The thought of him got to preying upon me every night; I could not get rid of it. I could not drive it away, the taking of that unoffending life seemed such a wanton thing. And it seemed an epitome of war, that all war must be just that—the killing of

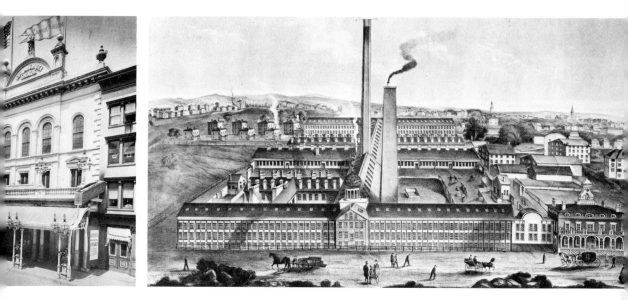

Left Ah Sin *opened and shortly after closed at Augustin Daly's Fifth Avenue Theater, New York.* Right *Colt's Patent Fire Arms Manufactory, Hartford. Lithograph by L. Schierholz, 1855*

strangers against whom you feel no personal animosity, strangers whom in other circumstances you would help if you found them in trouble, and who would help you if you needed it. My campaign was spoiled. It seemed to me that I was not rightly equipped for this awful business, that war was intended for men and I for a child's nurse.

In 1905, in 'The War Prayer', he was to write so savage an indictment of the martial spirit and of patriotic piety that he decided not to publish it within his lifetime. 'I have told the whole truth in that,' he said, 'and only dead men can tell the truth in this world.' The seeds of that bitter, prophetic parable of devastation and mourning are present in the light mockery of his speech to the patriots in October 1877: 'God protect the enemy.'

Another speech that Clemens gave that year, this one in Boston at a dinner on 17 December honoring the seventieth birthday of John Greenleaf Whittier, dogged him, on and off, for the rest of his life. Even thirty years later, contemplating the seating plan of the dinner at the Hotel Brunswick, he still recalled 'that disastrous cataclysm'. Its immediate aftermath had been an agony of shame and remorse aggravated by literary friends who magnified and even partly invented the disaster

—Howells's account of Clemens's 'hideous mistake', 'an effect of de-moniacal possession', verges on hysteria—and by newspaper references to an 'offense against good taste', evidence, as a hostile Massachusetts paper was saying almost ten years later, that 'Mr. Clemens . . . has no reliable sense of propriety.'

After the Chablis and the claret, the Mumm's Dry and the Roederer Imperial, Clemens rose to his feet and told a story in which Emerson, Holmes, and Longfellow—sacred cultural eminences and honored guests at the dinner—are grotesquely transformed. They appear as boozy tramps who in 1864, when the name Mark Twain was beginning to be known in California, invade a miner's cabin in the Sierra foothills and, spouting lines from their work all the while, drink up his whiskey, gorge themselves on his beans and bacon, cheat at cards, force him to sing 'When Johnny Comes Marching Home', and then make off with his only pair of boots. Soon after, Mark Twain, 'resolved to try the virtue of my *nom de guerre*', arrives at the cabin, identifies himself, and tries to explain things to the miner:

> 'Why, my dear sir, *these* were not the gracious singers to whom we and the world pay loving reverence and homage; these were impostors.'
>
> The miner investigated me with a calm eye for a while; then said he, 'Ah! impostors, were they? Are *you*?'

At the end of the speech, as Clemens persisted in recalling, his audience turned 'to stone with horror', as if 'I had been making these remarks about the Deity and the rest of the Trinity.' And this remembrance (considerably at variance with calmer reports of the evening), together with a pained and formal letter of apology to the gracious singers (who, with the exception of Emerson, in one of his chronic senile trances, had shown signs of mild amusement), seems as much the reflection of a guilty conscience as of a ghastly blunder. 'I do not ask you to forgive what I did that night, for it is not forgivable', he said in his letter. 'I simply had it at heart to ask you to believe that I am only heedlessly a savage, not premeditatedly.' More to the point might have been two quotations from the speech itself. 'Now I don't want to sass such famous littery people, but you see they kind of forced me,' the miner explains. 'I'm going to move; I ain't suited to a littery atmosphere.'

On 11 April 1878, Mr and Mrs Samuel Clemens of Hartford and their two daughters—Susy, six, and Clara, going on four—sailed from New York,

Opposite *Warwick Castle. 'Spent all day yesterday driving about Warwickshire in an open barouche.' Letter to Livy, 1872*

bound for Europe, on the steamship *Holsatia*. With them were an Elmira lady who had accompanied Livy to England five years earlier; a nurse-maid who was to give the children German lessons; and the Clemenses' Negro butler, who came along as valet and baggage agent. During the next year and a half this sizable traveling party was augmented by cicerones and couriers. It was in motive and spirit, not in scale of living or in itinerary, that Clemens departed from the pattern of upper-class Americans taking their domestic leisure abroad on a family grand tour of Germany, Switzerland, Italy, France, and England. He went to Europe partly in order to retreat from a string of professional mishaps, from the money- and energy-draining demands of the house in Hartford, from 'business responsibilities and annoyances, and the persecution of kindly letters from well-meaning strangers'. He also went as an intended expatriate who was at odds with many aspects of the national life as he saw it—political corruption, financial chicanery, a general air of venality, disorder, and demoralization—and who was therefore willing to reject it entirely in a mood as bleak and reactionary as that of Henry Adams.

Nook Farm itself, once a refuge, was divided and shaken in the aftermath of the Beecher scandal, and its fine fabric of sociability seemed to be crumbling along with the sanity of some of its leading citizens—Isabella Beecher Hooker was in a delusional state, her husband was afraid he was going mad, Calvin Stowe was visited by apparitions, and his wife, Harriet Beecher Stowe, was headed toward a schizoid anility in which she would go about frightening people out of their wits with 'her hideous gobblings and war whoops'. Outside Nook Farm, 1877 had been a year of violence which saw strikes by anthracite miners and railroad workers, pitched battles between militia and labor, rioting, pillage, and arson. Sixty thousand 'communists', someone told Clemens, were drilling in the streets of Cincinnati, Chicago, and St Louis, and armories were being hastily built to prepare for an expected rebellion led by anarchists and foreigners. All about him Mark Twain saw new, disturbing forces, which he barely understood or sympathized with then, but were surely changing the nation he thought he knew so well: the rise of organized labor; the wave of immigration, which during the next decade added over five million newcomers to a population of fifty million; the growth of cities and business combinations. Everything seemed to fan his old hatred for republican government, democracy, the vote, the jury system, and America in general.

Opposite *Our Brotherhood. Lithograph by The Strobridge Lithographic Co., 1885. The unionized worker. 'He is here—and he will remain. He is not a broken dam this time—he is the Flood!'*

Above *Labor violence, 1877. It was good 'to go and breathe the free air of Europe'.*
Notebook. Below *The Strike in the Coal Mines—Meeting of the 'Molly Maguire'
Men, 1874. The Molly Maguires were brought to trial in 1875*

It was 'good to go and breathe the free air of Europe', he wrote in his notebook on the way over, and he addressed his own country: 'I know you will refrain from saying harsh things *because* they can't hurt me, since I am out of reach and cannot hear them. That is why we say no harsh things of the dead.' Soon after he reached Germany he told Howells of his 'deep, grateful, unutterable sense of being "out of it all." I think I foretaste some of the advantages of being dead. Some of the joy of it.'

By contrast with his scandal-ridden country, Germany was a paradise, he exclaimed. 'What clean clothes, what good faces, what tranquil contentment, what prosperity, what genuine freedom, what superb government!' By contrast with Boston's chronically inhospitable atmosphere' Germany welcomed him as a favorite author. The Bostonian Thomas Wentworth Higginson (whose private opinion a few years earlier had been that Clemens was 'something of a buffoon') said in amazement, after visiting Koblenz in 1878: 'They all quote him before they have spoken with you fifteen minutes and always give him a place so much higher in literature than we do. I don't think any English prose writer is so universally read.' All of his books were available both in English and in German, a language which he loved but which baffled as well as delighted him by its intricacies. 'Yes, sir,' he noted, 'once the German language gets hold of a cat, it's goodbye cat', and he decided that he would rather decline two drinks than one German adjective.

It was in the flush of this requited love affair with Germany, German, and the Germans, that he sent an exuberant self-description to his friend Bayard Taylor, the American Minister in Berlin:

Geborn 1835; 5 Fuss 8½ inches hoch; weight doch aber about 145 pfund, sometimes ein wenig unter, sometimes ein wenig oben; dunkel braun Haar und rhotes Moustache, full Gesicht, mit sehr hohe Oren und leicht grau practvolles strahlenden Augen und ein Verdammtes gut moral character. Handlungkeit, Author von Bücher.

But Europe soon paled on him along with his first sense of relief at being out of America. He began to miss 'hot biscuits, *real* coffee with *real* cream—and *real* potatoes. Fried chicken, corn bread, *real* butter, *real* beefsteak, *good* roast beef with taste to it.' (As he was to say years later, the meat served on the Continent is 'as overdone as a martyr'.) He suffered temptations to suicide in plays and operas and, after considerable exposure, came to agree with Bill Nye that 'Wagner's music is better than it sounds.' *Lohengrin* was an extended 'insurrection', which caused him 'racking and pitiless pain'—'a great chorus composed entirely of maniacs would suddenly break forth, and then during two minutes, and sometimes three, I lived over again all that I had suffered the time the orphan asylum burned down'.

He grew to hate travel, hotels, old masters, and other features of life abroad so much that he was afraid he was too angry to write successful satire:

> I don't ever seem to be in a good enough humor with ANYthing to *satirize* it; no, I want to stand up before it & *curse* it, & foam at the mouth,—or take a club and pound it to rags & pulp.

His mood was further darkened by news of the imminent arrival, as American Consul at Krefeld, of Bret Harte, the only other American whose literary popularity could rival his in Germany. That his own government could actually 'send this nasty creature to puke upon the American name in a foreign land' disgusted him, he wrote to Howells, describing Harte as 'a liar, a thief, a swindler, a snob, a sot, a sponge, a coward. . . .' What had become a monomania after the disaster of *Ah Sin* was only to grow more violent with age.

The travel book Clemens had come over to write (published in 1880 as *A Tramp Abroad*) proved to be another uphill struggle, and he brought Twichell over for the summer of 1878 to keep him company on walking tours and sightseeing expeditions, to supply him with materials and a more genial point of view than his own, and in general to sweeten his mood. In the course of writing this travel book about middle-aged and middle-class tourists in Europe, Mark Twain worked a vein of more native materials. One episode—dealing with the confusion in odors of a decaying corpse, a box of limburger cheese, and a pile of burning chicken feathers, dried apples, rags, and old shoes—was in fact so close to the frontier mode that he decided to leave it out of the book altogether. Two brilliant chapters near the beginning of *A Tramp Abroad* deal with the California hermit Jim Baker, who understands the language of animals and birds and tells a story about a gullible bluejay. Toward the end of a digressive chapter there is a story about Nicodemus Dodge, a printer's apprentice in Hannibal, who had a skeleton put in his bed as a practical joke; the skeleton was that of Jimmy Finn, the town drunkard, who auctioned off first claim on it for fifty dollars—'The fifty dollars had gone promptly for whisky and had considerably hurried up the change of ownership in the skeleton.'

In the somewhat unexpected context of this European travel book there is a curious raft narrative, set on the river Neckar between Heilbronn and Heidelberg (one derivation of which is from a telescoping of *Heidelbeereberg*, meaning 'Huckleberry Mountain'). In various respects of mood—'The motion of a raft is the needful motion; it is

Left *Heidelberg: 'I used to sit for hours . . . watching the long, narrow rafts slip through the central channel.'* A Tramp Abroad. Right *Design for production of Wagner's* Das Rheingold, *Bayreuth, 1876*

gentle, and gliding, and smooth, and noiseless; it calms down all feverish activities'—and of resolution—the raft 'went all to smash and scatteration'—the narrative suggests that Mark Twain, as he waited for his tank to fill, was rehearsing by parody the parallel episode in *Huckleberry Finn* at which he had stopped work in 1876.

By the summer of 1879 even England had lost its hold over Mark Twain; he was certain now that the next century belonged to America. He was acutely bothered by the sensual arts of Italy and disgusted, to the point of obsession, by France. He described it as lacking winter, summer, and morals, a nation whose 'filthy-minded' citizens specialized in 'science and adultery', were the 'connecting link between man and monkey', and resembled no other tribe so much as the Comanches. Implicit in this invective, which filled page after page in his notebook, was a deep puzzlement, which he was never able to resolve satisfactorily in his work, and which went far beyond conventional double standards, over sexuality and censorship. (He could be the sternest and most fastidious of Victorians with his wife and daughters and at the same time give a comic and untrammeled speech to a men's group in Paris on the subject of the 'Science of Onanism'.) But also implicit in his invectives against the French was a contrast with his own country, which had begun to seem a model of civilization and morality. Mark Twain came home, gladly, in September 1879. The next time he went to Europe was in 1891, and then it was out of necessity, 'with rebellion in my heart, and bitterness'.

Paris: 'France is entitled to a distinguished place among the partly civilized people of our globe.' Letters from the Earth

He returned to America with the last stage in his 'desouthernization' complete, and instead of deriding the 'asinine government' of this 'leather-headed Republic' and looking forward to its downfall, he threw himself into the hurly-burly of public life as a professional Northerner, speechmaker for the Republican Party, and advance man for Ulysses S. Grant. The former President, considerably refurbished in standing by his absence from the White House and blazing again with some of the old heroic fire, had also returned from a long stay abroad and was to be welcomed home at a great banquet given in Chicago by the veterans of the Army of the Tennessee. Back in Elmira, struggling to finish *A Tramp Abroad*, Clemens felt the mighty appeal of the occasion—he compared it to the reunion of Napoleon and the Old Guard—and expressed it in terms which suggest that Grant was already an archangel in his imagination. 'My sluggish soul needs a fierce upstirring,' he told Howells, 'and if it does not get in when Grant enters the meeting place I must doubtless "lay" for the final resurrection.'

In Chicago, in November 1879, Mark Twain celebrated his reconciliation with America, joined his destiny to that of Grant, and also, by his own account, reached the high point of his career as speechmaker. Somewhat after two in the morning, Clemens climbed up on the banquet table at the Palmer House and responded to the toast he had devised for the occasion: 'The babies—as they comfort us in our sorrows, let us not forget them in our festivities.' By the end of his third sentence—

'When the toast works down to the babies, we stand on common ground' —he knew that the audience was his, and all the while watching Grant, who no longer wore his customary iron expression but laughed like the others, he marched through an elaborately double-edged tribute to the man of war, majestic on the battlefield but ridiculous in the nursery. He summoned up visions of the America of fifty years hence, a vast country whose leaders were now lying in their cradles.

It was worth risking everything to win an audience over, body and soul, he had once told Livy; now he led up to a climax, which threatened to turn into disaster. Relentlessly, with an apparent unawareness of the reverence in which his listeners held Grant, he described the future commander in chief of the American armies lying in his cradle and occupied with 'trying to find some way of getting his big toe in his mouth'. (Grant had, in fact, spent eight years in the Presidency trying to get his entire foot out.) This goal, Clemens went on, 'the illustrious guest of this evening turned his entire attention to some fifty-six years ago.' Here the laughter ceased, there was only 'a sort of shuddering silence', which he associated with the Whittier dinner, and then he sprang his masterful and stunning surprise: 'And if the child is but a prophecy of the man, there are mighty few who will doubt that he *succeeded.*'

Even Grant, 'laughed and cried like the mortalest of mortals', Clemens wrote in victory. 'I fetched him! I broke him up utterly. . . . I shook him up like dynamite.*. . . He laughed until his bones ached.' The former Marion Ranger was a hero of the evening, and the Army of the Tennessee was his to command, he was told. At noon that day he attended a breakfast in his honor given by some Chicago journalists, and he feasted on mushrooms, sweetbreads, quail, and cognac. 'Grand times, my boy,' he wrote to Howells, 'grand times.'

---

* Clemens seemed to describe his own method, as well as the implicit relationship of pain and humor, in his account of a visit to the dentist:

  At last the spindle stops whirling, and thundering in the cavity, and you know that the grand surprise is imminent, now—is hanging in the very air. You can hear your heart beat as the dentist bends over you with his grip on the spindle and his voice diminished to a murmur. The suspense grows bigger—bigger—bigger—your breath stops—then your heart. Then, with lightning suddenness, the 'nub' is sprung and the spindle drives into the raw nerve! The most brilliant surprises of the stage are pale and artificial compared with this' (*Europe and Elsewhere*, pp. 162–3.)

Chapter Five

'Everything a man could have'
1880–5

As a schoolboy admirer in Texas described him in 1880, Mark Twain, nearing forty-five, stood on the top rung of 'the ladder of fame' and had 'everything a man could have'—wealth, happiness, 'a beautiful wife and children', an envied domestic life. That summer Livy gave birth to their third daughter, Jean; Clara, born in 1874, was the only one who would survive her father; the eldest, Susy, born in 1872 shortly before the infant Langdon's death, was already idolized and claimed by her father with an intensity and extravagance that would later prove to be catastrophic. The children were tutored by Livy and a governess until they were old enough to go to Hartford Public High School, were kept away from parties, were accompanied wherever they went. They did not even attend such social fixtures as Sunday school, and at the age of five Susy recalled that she had been in a church only once, and that was to see her sister Clara christened or, as she said, 'crucified'. And when they grew up the girls observed and feared in their father a Victorian sternness, a determination, it seemed, to keep them away from men, away from the slightest imputation of coquetry.

But this austerity as far as public conduct was concerned contrasted with the private life of the Clemens household, intimate and demonstrative, and with their scale of living. By 1880 the expense of keeping up the Hartford house and providing champagne and fillets of beef for their guests added up to about as much as Mark Twain earned from royalties and investments. During 1881 he spent about one hundred thousand dollars in all, over thirty thousand of which went toward expanding and renovating 351 Farmington Avenue.

Opposite *Clara, Jean and Susy Clemens with their dog Hash, 1884*

Hartford Public High School, built 1869, destroyed 1882

Opposite *Cadets' Mess Hall, West Point. 'I knew more about retreating than the man that invented retreating.'*

Published in March 1880, *A Tramp Abroad*, Clemens's European travel book, sold sixty-two thousand copies during its first year in print. This was his greatest success since *The Innocents Abroad*, and it reversed a declining pattern of sales and popularity. Because he wanted it to be treated as a 'serious' book, he had once planned to conceal his authorship of *The Prince and the Pauper*, but when the book came out, over his name, in time for Christmas 1881, he reported with some relief that it 'is a great deal better received than I had any right to hope for'. Harriet Beecher Stowe, for one, was to tell him that it was 'the best book for young folks that was ever written', and this sort of praise was given canonical form in a full-length essay by William Dean Howells which appraised Mark Twain's total achievement and paid tribute to his moral fervor, 'the ethical intelligence' underlying his humor, and his strength and artistry as a storyteller. 'I hope the public will be willing to see me with your eyes', Clemens wrote to Howells. 'I shouldn't ask anything better than that.'

'After twenty-one years' absence,' he was to write in *Life on the Mississippi*, 'I felt a very strong desire to see the river again, and the steamboats, and such of the boys as might be left; so I resolved to go out there.' The first half of his river book, consisting mainly of the seven articles he wrote for the *Atlantic* in 1875, celebrates learning, adventure, and the glory of steamboating as he had known them before the Civil War. The second half is a report of his return to the river in the spring of 1882, and

it reflects quite another mood, together with a conviction that he shared with Howells, Whitman, Henry Adams, and other writers of the time, that after the war something precious and redeeming left American life and was replaced by hardness and cynicism, the lust for money and the worship of money. This was the theme of *The Gilded Age* and Mark Twain's later utterances as moralist and social critic.

Even before he reached St Louis in April 1882, Mark Twain was prepared for strangeness and loss. The South, *his* South, he was certain, subsisted on juvenile fantasies of heroism and chivalry, was backward and poverty stricken, and he already knew it as a present fact that the railroads had killed off traffic on the Mississippi. At the St Louis levee, once packed solid with steamboats, he found only half a dozen, their fires banked or dead. Even the sight of a steamboat named *Mark Twain* did not relieve the general air of strangeness and desolation that he found as he traveled down river to New Orleans. The river was different, too, 'as brand new as if it had been built yesterday', and all that remained of his pilot knowledge was a landsman's skill in remembering names and addresses. On the return trip he arrived at Hannibal on a still Sunday morning. The town seemed deserted. 'Everything was changed, but when I reached Third or Fourth street the tears burst forth, for I recognized the mud.' And he felt that morning like a prisoner seeing Paris again after years of captivity in the Bastille.

Clemens's six-week trip of hail and farewell to Hannibal and the

Left *'We met two steamboats at New Madrid. Two steamboats in sight at once! An infrequent spectacle.'* Life on the Mississippi. Right *'I seemed to have forgotten the river, but I hadn't forgotten how to steer a steamboat, nor how to enjoy it, either.'* Life on the Mississippi

river gave him material and impetus for more than a year and a half of productive work on two books: *Life on the Mississippi*, begun eight years earlier as a serial for the *Atlantic*, and *Huckleberry Finn*, begun six years earlier and which he was now describing as 'a story which details some passages in the life of an ignorant village boy, Huck Finn, son of the town drunkard of my time out West'. Almost the whole of Chapter 3 of *Life on the Mississippi* is the raftsmen's chapter ('illustrating keelboat talk and manners') from the novel, seven thousand words or so, and there are other substantial borrowings, overlappings, and evidences of cross-pollination. He made progress on the novel while finishing his river book. 'I never had such a fight . . . in my life before,' he said about *Life on the Mississippi*—'this wretched God-damned book', a disappointment to him when it was finally published in May 1883. It was to be years before the new book sold anywhere near the one hundred thousand copies he expected it to sell right away. Even so, *Life on the Mississippi* fitted into a constellation of favoring circumstances—an opulent present and a transfigured past—under which Mark Twain worked at Quarry Farm during the euphoric summer of 1883.

126

'I haven't had such booming working-days for many years', he reported to his mother and Orion that July—'I am piling up manuscript in a really astonishing way. I believe I shall complete, in two months, a book which I have been fooling over for 7 years. This summer it is no more trouble to me to write than it is to lie.' He had reached the high point of his life as a writer of fiction. That summer, often writing three or four thousand words at a sitting, he finished *Huckleberry Finn* and was no longer tentative about it, as he had been in 1876. It was 'rattling good', he now said, and he even anticipated with confidence the troubled reception the book was to have: '*I* shall *like* it, whether anybody else does or not.'

That summer he was so intoxicated with the plenitude of his creative energies that he was capable of having the blind staggers about what he was up to. A few years earlier he had scolded Orion for fickleness and vagrancy of purpose, for being a kaleidoscope instead of a telescope; he had declared solemnly, 'The bane of Americans is overwork—and the ruin of *any* work is a divided interest. Concentrate—*concentrate*.' Now he himself was concentrating, more or less simultaneously, on his masterpiece in fiction, *Huckleberry Finn*, and a project which Howells told him frankly was not even 'your second-best', a numbing continuation of the *Arabian Nights* in which Scheherazade talks King Shahryar to death along with the reader; a burlesque account of the Second Coming and a play in which a lunatic equipped with wings and a fire extinguisher capers around the stage; various business ventures, the smallest of which then was a plan to manufacture some grape scissors invented by Howells's father and the largest of which was a growing involvement with publishing which culminated in Mark Twain's fatal decision to publish his own books; and a history game which he originally designed for his three adored daughters to play on the long driveway at Quarry Farm, but was soon translated, characteristically, into a vendible board game which he believed would sweep the world and bring him a fortune. All things seemed possible that summer. The future was open, and for Mark Twain, living, creating, and speculating to the hilt in 'the raging, tearing, booming nineteenth century', the glorious age of steam, electricity, and progress, history was still only a 'game'.

Although it was mild compared with the panics and depressions of 1873 and 1893, the financial crisis of 1884, a 'little' panic, had a decisive effect on Mark Twain's life. 'Losses, ill luck, and botched business' had rocked him out of his accustomed prosperity, and he was forced to take to the road again, with the Southern novelist George Washington Cable as his partner. 'I want good company on the road and at the hotels', he explained to a reporter. 'A man can start out alone and rob the public, but it's dreary work and a cold-blooded thing to do.' This time he was impresario as well as a performer who was teaching himself a new performing skill. For the vogue had shifted from the humorous lecture, which had taken him years to master, to the author's reading, an attraction first popularized in America by Charles Dickens. Now in order to create the illusion of a man telling and partly acting out a story (including several episodes from advance sheets of *Huckleberry Finn*), Clemens had to modify as well as memorize the printed page. His tour with Cable—the two of them were billed as 'Twins of Genius'— opened in New Haven in November 1884 and, after a hundred and four performances, ten thousand miles of travel, and months of homeless nights in the hotels of seventy cities, closed in Washington at the end of February 1885.

The tour wore him out in spirit and patience, drove him to tantrums, demeaning feuds with Cable, and fits of depression and self-loathing during which he felt he had allowed himself to become 'a mere buffoon'. But he had earned seventeen thousand dollars and discovered a new area of seeming invincibility to which he would return ten years later, when he was working his way out of bankruptcy. He had perfected a platform manner which appeared to be utterly natural, like the speech rhythms and idiomatic flow of his writing, but was a triumph of control and artifice. He lounged about the stage, coughed dryly from time to time, pulled at his mustache, and even seemed to be on the edge of falling asleep just before he sprang those nubs, snappers, and surprises that made his audiences 'jump out of their skins', as he told Livy. Then, as before at the Grant banquet in Chicago, his ears rang with 'a long roll of artillery laughter' punctuated by 'Congreve rockets and bomb- shell explosions'.

Well before the end of the tour, Clemens's fortunes had become fatally intertwined with those of another, more celebrated victim of the panic of 1884. That May, Ulysses Grant's stock-exchange firm went bankrupt, and at sixty-two the former Union commander and eighteenth President of the United States found that he had been picked so clean he could hardly pay his butcher bill. Now, like other military and political heroes before and after him, his chief assets were his memoirs, a project that he and Clemens had casually talked about in fatter days. Now it had a grim urgency. The General saw no other way of keeping his

Opposite 'Twins of Genius': with George Washington Cable, 1884

family out of the poorhouse; and Clemens, who had just set up his nephew Charley Webster in business to handle, among other business ventures, *Huckleberry Finn*, was determined to perform a double act of piety and commerce by publishing Grant. 'I wanted the General's book,' he said, 'and I wanted it very much.' He got it, too, after strenuous wooing, but he thereby became, in eventual terms, a party to his own undoing. For the Grant bonanza, as it proved to be, encouraged Clemens to go on to bigger and bigger business ventures—'excesses of enterprise', Howells called them—which debilitated him as a writer, came close to destroying him as a man, and brought him into bankruptcy.

But this denouement was still years away when, in the autumn of 1885, Clemens published *Personal Memoirs of U. S. Grant* in two volumes and delighted in calculating the dimensions of his gigantic success: a sale of over two hundred thousand sets, royalties to the Grant family of nearly half a million dollars (or, as he rendered it, seventeen tons of silver coin), and a profit of two hundred thousand dollars and more for the firm of Charles L. Webster and Company of New York, publishers also of *The Adventures of Huckleberry Finn.*

In time Mark Twain's new book would be read in millions of copies printed in nearly every tongue, and even critics who quarreled over whether its ending was appropriate, disastrous, or practically beneath mention would not seriously question whether the book was literature. 'It's the best book we've had', Ernest Hemingway wrote in 1938 in *Green Hills of Africa.* 'All American writing comes from that. There was nothing before.' But during the winter and spring of 1885 *Huckleberry Finn*—'a book of mine where a sound heart and a deformed conscience come into collision and conscience suffers defeat'—seemed to offer its author-publisher a lesson in the vindictiveness of entrenched orthodoxy. On 10 February 1885, a week before publication, Clemens told his nephew, 'I am not able to see that anything can save Huck Finn from being another defeat.' There was not even the prospect of a favorable review of any influence or importance, and it was not until May, in the *Century*, that the scholar and critic Thomas Sergeant Perry discussed *Huckleberry Finn* as 'a vivid picture of Western life of forty or fifty years ago' and praised its 'immortal hero'.

Later in the year Joel Chandler Harris, the creator of Uncle Remus, concluded a public letter of praise for *Huckleberry Finn* with the pointed acknowledgment that 'some of the professional critics will not agree with me'. For what the professional critics were saying, when they said anything, was more nearly typified in the comic magazine *Life*, which

Opposite *Bird's Eye View of New Orleans. Lithograph by Currier and Ives, 1885*

savagely attacked *Huckleberry Finn* for its 'blood-curdling humor', gutter realism, 'coarse and dreary fun', and total unsuitability for young people. Ironically, Clemens had taken especial pains to forestall charges of coarseness and impropriety. He rejected several proposed illustrations, with extremist censorial severity, as too 'violent', 'forbidding', 'repulsive', or 'disgusting'. Despite these precautions, a kind of wicked justice came close to prevailing: Charles L. Webster and Company postponed publication at the last moment, and thereby missed the Christmas trade of 1884, when it was discovered that a mischievous engraver had made indecent alterations in the printing plate of one of the illustrations. And despite his aversion to proofreading and self-editing, Clemens combed through the text carefully; asked Howells (who was distinctly prudish) to go over the manuscript and some of the proofs; and then gave Livy the page proofs to 'expergate' (Susy's revealing word for the editorial act in general).

Clemens popularized and elaborated a myth that Livy was his strictest censor, but in fact her standards of decorum were considerably more liberal than those of Richard Watson Gilder of the *Century*. Gilder, in editing selections from *Huckleberry Finn* for his magazine, bowdlerized references to nakedness, blasphemy, smells, and dead cats, and even changed 'in a sweat' to 'in such a hurry'. The process of bowdlerizing *Huckleberry Finn* still goes on, although the criteria for what is objectionable have changed. In a recent high-school text, 'nigger woman' becomes 'one of the servants', while 'a young white gentleman' becomes 'a young gentleman'. The spirit of *Huckleberry Finn*, its intention, and indeed the entire difference between literature and propaganda may be no better understood now than they were in 1885.

By the standards of 1885, and by subsequent standards as well, *Huckleberry Finn* was an outlaw book.* In contrast with the nerveless, bookish prose of *The Prince and the Pauper* and, later, *Joan of Arc*, *Huckleberry Finn* was in part 'a language experiment' (one of Walt

---

* '*Huckleberry Finn* was once barred from certain libraries and schools for its alleged subversion of morality. The authorities had in mind the book's endemic lying, the petty thefts, the denigrations of respectability and religion, the bad language, and the bad grammar. We smiled at that excessive care; yet, in point of fact, *Huckleberry Finn* is indeed a subversive book—no one who reads thoughtfully the dialectic of Huck's great moral crisis will ever again be wholly able to accept without some question and some irony the assumptions of the respectable morality by which he lives, or will ever again be certain that what he considers the clear dictates of moral reason are not merely the engrained customary beliefs of his time and place.' (Lionel Trilling, *The Liberal Imagination* [Garden City, N. Y.: Doubleday, 1957], p. 108.)

Opposite *Nearing the Issue at the Cockpit by Horace Bonham, 1870. 'I never saw people enjoy anything more.'* Life on the Mississippi

Whitman's characterizations of *Leaves of Grass*). 'In this book', Mark Twain said in his explanatory note at the very start,

> a number of dialects are used to wit: the Missouri negro dialect; the extremest form of the backwoods South-Western dialect; the ordinary 'Pike-County' dialect; and four modified varieties of this last. The shadings have not been done in a hap-hazard fashion, or by guess-work; but pains-takingly, and with the trustworthy guidance and support of personal familiarity with these several forms of speech.
>
> I make this explanation for the reason that without it many readers would suppose that all these characters were trying to talk alike and not succeeding.

Joel Chandler Harris, creator of Uncle Remus. The children 'were grievously disappointed to find he was white and young'. Letter to Livy, 1882

Opposite *The Grant funeral procession, Fifth Avenue and 41st Street, New York, 8 August 1885*

In his exploration of the literary possibilities of dialect, Mark Twain went far beyond Cable, Joel Chandler Harris, and other local colorists of his time, although he was indebted to them for showing the way. Dialect became naturalized in *Huckleberry Finn* and the English language broadened and invigorated thereby into something altogether new in narrative prose and altogether native, a written, literary medium with the rhythms, freedom, and color of American colloquial speech. (Mark Twain used English, Howells said admiringly, 'as if it

had come up out of American, out of Missourian ground'.) This vernacular shapes the vision and passion of the book, for it is not 'Mr Mark Twain', the narrator of *Tom Sawyer* ('he told the truth, mainly'), who now tells Huck's story, but Huck Finn himself. As he undergoes an education of his sound heart through his adventures on the river and along its shores, Huck ultimately passes judgment on society and its supporting assumptions of right and wrong. For all his boyishness and generosity Huck is shrewder, and a more adversary and rebellious figure, than even the rapscallion Duke and Dauphin, who reach derisive conclusions of their own—'Hain't we got all the fools in town on our side? and ain't that a big enough majority in any town?'

The spokesmen for the genteel tradition, who had praised *The Prince and the Pauper*, turned their back on the book which sprang from Mark Twain's most powerful imperatives. Troubled in goal and standard, he was to look back on *Huckleberry Finn* with mingled pain, pride, and puzzlement, and even say, in later years, that his favorite among all his books was *Joan of Arc*. In 1885 he described his masterpiece to Joel Chandler Harris as 'Huck, that abused child of mine who has had so much unfair mud slung at him. Somehow, I can't help believing in him.' It was to be four and a half years before he published his next book, *A Connecticut Yankee in King Arthur's Court*, and he said that this book—in which he translated into a fantasy of warfare some of the antagonisms he had experienced between vernacular and genteel values—was going to be his swan song, his 'retirement from literature permanently'. He was going to make sure that 'those parties who miscall themselves critics' would not have a chance to 'paw the book at all'—'I wish to pass to the cemetery unclodded.'

By the time he published *A Connecticut Yankee* in 1889 he had begun to see more hope and reward for himself in business than in the practice of literature. In view of his subsequent history of broken business hopes, there could scarcely be a more poignant understatement than the bibliographical entry for the year 1890 in Albert Bigelow Paine's biography: 'No important literary matters this year. Mark Twain engaged in promoting the Paige typesetting machine.' The only literary matter Paine lists for that year is a long letter to the English critic

Opposite Above left *E. W. Kemble's frontispiece for* The Adventures of Huckleberry Finn. Above right *In the cave. '"Jim, this is nice," I says. "I wouldn't want to be nowhere else but here."'* Illustration from Huckleberry Finn. Below *'"Huckleberry Finn" was Tom Blankenship,' who lived in this Hannibal house. 'Tom's father was at one time Town Drunkard, an exceedingly well-defined and unofficial office of those days.'* Autobiography

Andrew Lang in which Mark Twain seems almost to be generalizing from the painful career of *Huckleberry Finn*, by then a critical failure but a popular success, and appealing for some apter standard:

> Indeed I have been misjudged from the very first. I have never tried in even one single little instance to help cultivate the cultivated classes. I was not equipped for it, either by native gifts or training. And I never had any ambition in that direction, but always hunted for bigger game—the masses. . . . Yes, you see, I have always catered for the Belly and the Members but have been served like the others—criticized from the culture standard—to my sorrow and pain; because, honestly, I never cared what became of the cultured classes; they could go to the theatre and the opera, they had no use for me and the melodeon.

Mark Twain's own troublement over *Huckleberry Finn* was mirrored within his family. Livy was fond of 'dear old Huck', but was never comfortable with the book. Susy disapproved. She believed that her father was a great man, but she preferred that he demonstrate his greatness in some more orthodox manner, as if he were the defective timepiece which in 1885 he sent back to the jewelers with this characteristic note: 'Dear Sirs—The watch which Mrs. Clemens bought of you some days ago keeps too much time, sometimes, and the rest of the time it doesn't keep

Nearing fifty. The picture was probably taken for private circulation and amusement

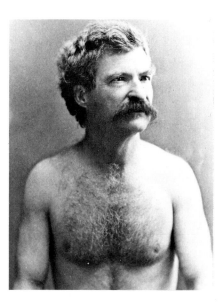

any. Will you please take out its present works and put in some of a more orthodox character. Yours truly, S. L. Clemens.'

For nearly a month after publication, *Huckleberry Finn* existed in a kind of critical outer darkness. Then, one day in March, the Library Committee of Concord, Massachusetts, pronounced the book coarse and inelegant, and expelled it from the library shelves. 'If Mr. Clemens cannot think of something better to tell our pure-minded lads and lasses,' said Louisa May Alcott in a statement echoed in the New England press, 'he had best stop writing for them.' Through all this, despite his private rage against 'those idiots in Concord', Clemens managed to present to his public the image of a confident, masterful, and good-humored author who not only was going to endure this series of affronts but also was going to make the most of it by exploiting the rewards of being banned in (or near) Boston.

'Dear Charley,' Clemens wrote on 18 March in a letter which he released to the newspapers,

> The Committee of the Public Library of Concord, Mass., have given us a rattling tip-top puff which will go into every paper in the country. They have expelled Huck from their library as 'trash and suitable only for the slums.' That will sell 25,000 copies for us sure.

At the end of the month he released a second letter, which pointed out other ways in which he was going to benefit from the Concord excommunication:

> For instance, it will deter other libraries from buying the book and you are doubtless aware that one book in a public library prevents the sale of a sure ten and a possible hundred of its mates. And secondly it will cause the purchasers of the book to read it, out of curiosity, instead of merely intending to do so after the usual way of the world and library committees; and then they will discover, to my great advantage and their own indignant disappointment, that there is nothing objectionable in the book, after all.

Soon, instead of 'another defeat', Mark Twain saw that *Huckleberry Finn* was going to be a 'handsome success' in the face of official indifference and active disapproval. There was every indication that it would never stop being bought and read.

CATALOGUE A.

OTT, MERGENTHALER AND CO.

BALTIMORE, MD.

MECHANICAL ENGINEERS AND MACHINISTS.

LINOTYPE PARTS.

LINOTYPE ATTACHMENTS.

LINOTYPE SUPPLIES

LINOTYPE IMPROVEMENTS.

INVENTORS

LINOTYPE.

AND MANUFACTURERS OF THE

LINOTYPE OFFICE IMPLEMENTS.

REPAIRING OF LINOTYPE MACHINES.

REPAIRING OF LINOTYPE MACHINE PARTS.

REPAIRING OF LINOTYPE SPACE BANDS.

DEALING IN SECOND HAND LINOTYPE MACHINES.

CABLE ADDRESS: LINOTYPE, BALTIMORE.

WE MAKE A SPECIALTY OF DESIGNING AND BUILDING AUTOMATIC MACHINERY OF EVERY DESCRIPTION, SPECIAL TOOLS, MODELS, ETC.

Chapter Six

'One dear project of mine'
1886–96

In 1880 Mark Twain made a first investment of five thousand dollars in an automatic typesetting machine that was being built at the Colt arms factory in Hartford under the supervision of its inventor, James W. Paige. Even at an early stage of development, Paige's machine, with one operator seated at its keyboard, did the work of four men setting type by hand. Until he saw it in action, Mark Twain, who never forgot his own years of drudgery holding a composing stick, had not believed that such a machine could exist, but soon after he saw it and fell under Paige's spell, he began to celebrate this 'mechanical marvel' which made 'all the other wonderful inventions of the human brain'—he cited the telephone, telegraph, locomotive, cotton gin, sewing machine, Babbage calculator, Jacquard loom, perfecting press, and Arkwright frame—'sink pretty nearly into commonplace' and seem 'mere toys, simplicities'.

In actuality, *The Times* of London had been experimenting with automatic typesetters and typecasters for years, and meanwhile, in Baltimore, Ottmar Mergenthaler was perfecting his Linotype machine, which eliminated direct typesetting altogether and became one of the chief technological advances of the century. Mark Twain, as it turned out, had fully understood the implications and potentials of mechanical composition. He devoted about fifteen years and two hundred thousand dollars to Paige's machine, using, in addition, his publishing house as a private bank to finance it. His mistake was in backing the wrong horse in a race for the right purse. For Paige's machine, which eventually comprised about eighteen thousand separate parts, was impossibly delicate and temperamental, having been conceived, apparently, as an organism rather than a machine. Its life history had to be written as a

James W. Paige's 'inspired', 'cunning', and 'magnificent' typesetting machine in its present home, the basement of Mark Twain's house

series of progressively more costly breakdowns, delays, and 'improvements'. And all the while, Paige and his chief backer, before exposing their mechanical marvel to the hazards of the market place, insisted on bringing it to 'a perfection so expensive', Howells recalled, 'that it was practically impracticable'.

Nevertheless, in February 1886, after six years of feeding Paige and the machine out of his pocket, Mark Twain went on to a bigger scheme than before and organized a company to perfect, manufacture, and market the typesetter all over the world. At precisely the same time, after a year of almost total involvement with publishing affairs, and especially the Grant *Memoirs,* he returned to full-time writing with *A Connecticut Yankee in King Arthur's Court*, the tale of a Hartford master mechanic—superintendent at the same Colt factory where the typesetter was being built—who, after suffering a severe blow on the head, wakes up near Camelot, in sixth-century England.

Mark Twain began his story as an apparently straightforward burlesque elaboration of Sir Thomas Malory's *Morte d'Arthur*, a book Cable had introduced him to when they were on tour together. 'You'll never lay it down until you have read it from cover to cover', Cable promised, and even despite later recriminations that often threatened

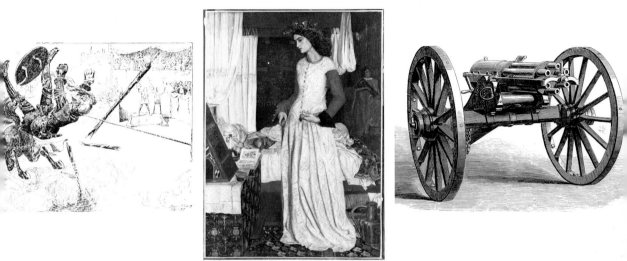

Left *'The next moment the rope sprang taut and yanked Sir Sagramour out of the saddle! Great Scott, but there was a sensation!' Illustration by Dan Beard for* A Connecticut Yankee. *Centre* Queen Guinevere *by William Morris, 1858.* Right *Gatling Gun, a product of the Colt factory in Hartford*

to turn their relationship into a public scandal, Clemens freely and gratefully acknowledged that Cable was the 'godfather' of *A Connecticut Yankee*. For shortly after reading Malory, Clemens made his first note for the new book:

> Dream of being a knight errant in armor in the middle ages. Have the notions and habits of thought of the present day mixed with the necessities of that. No pockets in the armor. No way to manage certain requirements of nature. Can't scratch. Cold in the head—can't blow—can't get at handkerchief, can't use iron sleeve. Iron gets red hot in the sun—leaks in the rain, gets white with frost and freezes me solid in winter. Suffer from lice and fleas. Make disagreeable clatter when I enter church. Can't dress or undress myself. Always getting struck by lightning. Fall down, can't get up.

From the very start the dream about knight errantry had been joined in Mark Twain's mind by another idea:

> Have a battle between modern army with gatling guns—(automatic) 600 shots a minute, with one pulling of the trigger, torpedos, balloons, 100-ton cannon, ironclad fleet &c & Prince de Joinville's Middle Age Crusaders.

(Among this array of 'labor-saving machinery', the Gatling gun was yet another product of the Colt Patent Fire Arms Manufacturing Company of peaceable Hartford.)

Between February 1886, when he began *A Connecticut Yankee*, and May 1889, when he finished it, these germ ideas—burlesques and extravaganzas of a sort that came almost by instinct to Mark Twain—changed their course. They veered away from laughter toward the final 'Battle of the Sand-Belt', an apocalyptic conclusion which Henry Nash Smith has called 'one of the most distressing passages in American literature': Mark Twain's way of resolving the conflicts of his book proved to be a massacre in which past and present, Arthur's feudal society and the Yankee's industrial republic, destroy one another. It seems likely, then, that in addition to its burlesque surface, the germ idea suggested other directions which are more consistent with the way Mark Twain carried it forward.* One could conceivably say that the dream of being a knight errant in armor is at the same time a nightmare of being swaddled in iron, confined and helpless, just as Mark Twain, author of *Huckleberry Finn* and emerging social critic, often felt confined, helpless, and angry in the society which both embraced and rejected him. One would be on safer ground saying that the dream, or nightmare, is explicitly a form of time travel, a narrative and imaginative mode peculiarly appropriate to Mark Twain's concerns and those of his contemporaries.

'You know about transmigration of souls', the Yankee says, introducing his strange history. 'Do you know about transposition of epochs —and bodies?' Mark Twain himself, though glorying in the present and in his sense of possession, sometimes felt as dislocated in time as the Yankee: his Hannibal was the Yankee's Camelot. He had been born into the feudal, slaveholding culture of the agrarian South. Industrialism, the railroad, the discovery of gold at Sutter's Mill, and finally the Civil War had changed the world of his boyhood. He had already seen the passing of the stagecoach, the Pony Express, and the glory of steamboating on the Mississippi. Now, blessed by technological wonders like the telephone and the high-speed printing press, he lived in an industrial nation fast becoming urbanized, wholly given over to the

---

* 'That notion of yours about the Hartford man waking up in King Arthur's time is capital', Howells said in 1886, after he heard the story talked to him, and even in 1908, when he was reading *A Connecticut Yankee* for at least the second time, he called it 'the most delightful, truest, most humane, sweetest fancy that ever was', a judgment almost bizarrely unresponsive to the fact that the book ends with a disaster and that there are hints of mayhem and apocalypse all the way through it. In general, as the psychologist Robert Sears commented in 1961, 'The reading public seems to have ignored the underlying message with such deliberate success as to make one speculate favorably on the human race's capacity for avoiding pain.'

Yankee values of trade and production, and subject to the inexorable process of moral erosion which he associated with money. Sometimes Mark Twain felt like the oldest man in the world, one of the vestiges of creation.

Visiting Hannibal in January 1885, just when he was under the spell of Malory, Clemens had felt himself swept under by 'infinite great deeps of pathos', by waves of helpless longing for a lost Eden and his boyhood there. His distance from the receding past was symbolized for him by the pathetic figure of his 'cradle-mate, baby-mate, little boy-mate', Tom Nash, deaf and dumb now as he had been for almost forty years, since the night he went skating with Sam and fell into the river.

Caricature by Theodore Wust, 1890–5

Sam's mother too, with whom he spent 'a beautiful evening' of reminiscence, was increasingly dislocated from the present; she was eighty-two now and would live five more years of increasing remoteness and abstraction. 'Poor old Ma,' he noted, 'asking in haste for news about people who have been dead forty, fifty, and sixty years.' Like Jane Clemens, sinking so far and fast into anility that soon she would have to ask Orion what relation Sam was to her, the Yankee, even as first conceived, has lost the power and desire to shake off his dream. 'He mourns his lost land—has come to England and revisited it, but it is all so changed and become old, so old—and it was so fresh and new, so virgin before.' Thus Clemens outlined the frame story surrounding Hank Morgan's yellowed palimpsest, and he supplied the only possible ending: 'He has lost all interest in life—is found dead next morning—suicide.'

Clemens's vestigial mood was enforced by visions of scientific and social progress, by the vistas of time opened up by evolutionary thought and by 'the great Darwin', whom he had visited in 1879 (and who was one of his devoted readers), and by such excursions into ancient history as Heinrich Schliemann's excavation at Troy, Mycenae, and Ithaca during the 1870s. Given this enlarging time scale, Mark Twain could look back on his boyhood in Hannibal and feel the same paradox of change and continuity as Henry Adams, an eighteenth-century man, by his own account, who was born into the nineteenth and survived well into the twentieth. Adams mused by Wenlock Edge on the eons of time that separated him from, linked him to, the ganoid fish and the horseshoe crab.

Other writers of Mark Twain's time, responding to the same evolutionary and historical perspectives, were turning to fables of time travel to express a sense of wonder, contrast, and possibility. In 1885, just as Mark Twain began *A Connecticut Yankee*, H. Rider Haggard, the popular romancer, published *King Solomon's Mines*, a story about contemporary Englishmen who discover an ancient, surviving Judaeo-African civilization; Haggard's novel of adventure has a number of extraordinarily close and suggestive parallels to Mark Twain's.* In 1887 Haggard published *She*, a confrontation of Pharaonic and Victorian cultures which deals principally in what the Yankee would call 'transmigration of souls', 'transposition of epochs—and bodies'. The same year the American Edward Bellamy brought out *Looking Backward* and from the imagined vantage point of AD 2000 presented a vigorous critique of the social and political problems of the 1880s. In 1894, a nightmare year of depression and unemployment in America, William Dean Howells described Utopian alternatives to capitalism in *A Traveler from Altruria*, while in England the young H. G. Wells published *The Time Machine*, which he described as 'a fantasy based on the idea of the human species developing along divergent lines'. *The Time Machine* was the first of

---

* Among these parallels are: the encounter of a modern technological culture (as represented by guns, primarily) with an ancient ceremonial culture; the figure of the wicked shaman who represents magic as well as religious orthodoxy; a solar eclipse which serves as an occasion for modern man to translate his scientific knowledge into a magical power; a love affair between a man of the modern culture and a girl of the ancient; and finally a great battle which destroys the ancient culture.

Wells's several treatments of a problem posed, as he said in his auto-biography, 'by an age of material progress and political sterility'. This problem, translated to Arthurian England, was one of the central concerns of Mark Twain's new book.

In the course of its writing, *A Connecticut Yankee* became an extravagant, savagely conflictive book, at the same time an entertainment and a dark anarchic fable, a comic romance and a work of profoundly troubled commentary which anticipates the social and political criticism that was, along with his autobiography, the distinctive glory of the last decade of Mark Twain's life. *A Connecticut Yankee* is a lexicon of the concerns of its era and also, as Henry Nash Smith has said, 'a central document in American intellectual history'. The two opposed currents of Mark Twain's life flow through the book: its hilarity, compassion, benign fantasy, and nostalgia for a lost time correspond to an underlying puzzlement, desperation, and anger with the present. His period of 'Anglomania' was behind him, and now in his story of jousting and spells he seemed to be feuding with English history and character, with the hallowed body of Arthurian legend and tradition, and with such

Haymarket Square riot, Chicago, 4 May 1886

guardians of high culture as Matthew Arnold. Arnold had deplored the lack of distinction in America, the lack of 'what is elevated and beautiful, of what is interesting', and, much as if he were pointing at Mark Twain, had even gone out of his way to denigrate the prose style of Ulysses S. Grant and to deplore the popularity in America of the 'funny man' as a 'national misfortune'.

'The change is in *me*—in my vision of the evidences', Clemens told Howells in August 1887. He had been rereading Thomas Carlyle's *The French Revolution*, the favorite book that was to lie beside him on his deathbed. He now recognized that 'life and environment' had made him a revolutionary, 'a Sansculotte!—And not a pale, characterless Sansculotte but a Marat', pitted against all forms of tyranny and oppression and committed to direct action. 'If such a government cannot be overthrown otherwise than by dynamite', Mark Twain exclaimed after hearing the traveler and lecturer George Kennan describe life under Czar Alexander III, 'then thank God for dynamite'. Attempts on the Czar's life were among other 'evidences' that ancient forms of authority were falling. The 1880s in America saw the rise of the trade unions: the Knights of Labor reached a membership of seven hundred thousand; the American Federation of Labor was founded. 'In the Unions', Mark Twain believed, 'was the working-man's only present hope of standing up like a man against money and the power of it . . . the sole present help of the weak against the strong.' The Haymarket riot in Chicago in 1886 and its aftermath showed how bitterly opposed these forces could be.

When the Emperor of Brazil, Dom Pedro II, was overthrown at the end of 1889, Mark Twain rejoiced. 'These are immense days! Republics and rumors of republics, from everywhere in the earth', he said, and in advance of the publication of *A Connecticut Yankee* he proposed to publish extracts from the book 'that have in them this new breath of republics'. And yet what the Yankee dynamites at the end of his story is not only autocratic Europe, as symbolized by feudalism, but also all the apparatus of the democratic 'new deal' he had tried to impose on what he now bitterly acknowledges to be 'human muck'.

For about three years the Yankee and Paige's typesetter were twinned in Mark Twain's mind. 'I want to finish the day the machine finishes', he kept saying of his new book, tacitly acknowledging an occult relationship between a writer writing words and a machine ('a cunning devil', he called it, a 'magnificent creature') setting them in type. Both the book

Opposite *The Eglinton Tournament, Ayrshire, 1839. 'Just a little wearisome to the practical mind.'* A Connecticut Yankee

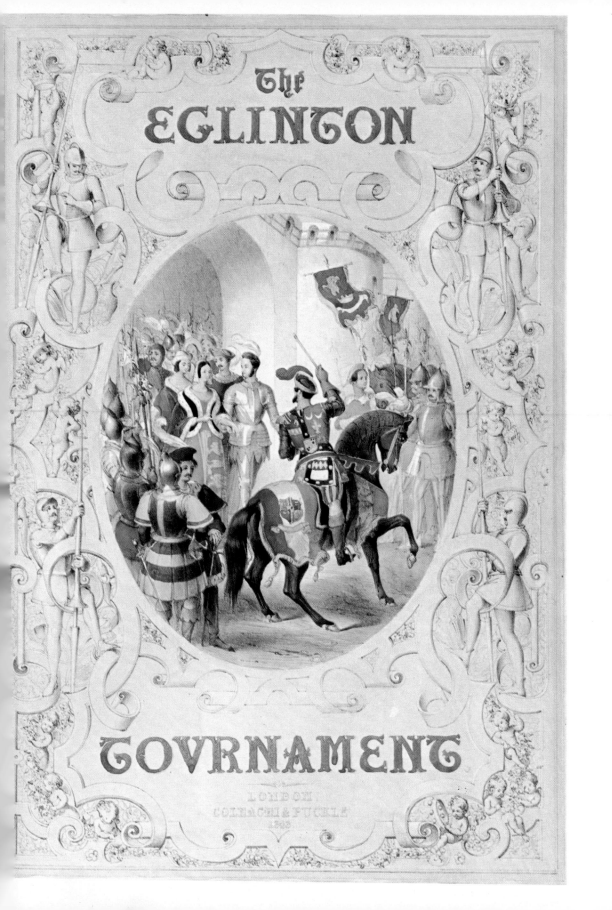

The
EGLINTON
TOVRNAMENT

LONDON
COLNAGHI & PUCKLE
1843

and the machine were tests of his century's faith in democracy, tech-
nology, progress, the entrepreneurial motive, and the gospel of success,
and he was soon to make it clear that what had been at stake for him in
the typesetter was not just a business venture but an entire framework
of aspiration:

> . . . I watched over one dear project of mine five years, spent a fortune on it,
> and failed to make it go—and the history of that would make a large book in
> which a million men would see themselves as in a mirror: and they would
> testify and say, Verily this is not imagination, this fellow has been there—
> and after would they cast dust upon their heads, cursing and blaspheming.

He made a parallel statement about *A Connecticut Yankee* when he
finished it:

> If it were only to write over again there wouldn't be so many things left out.
> They burn in me; and they keep multiplying; but now they can't ever be
> said. And besides, they would require a library—and a pen warmed up in hell.

By the summer of 1887 Mark Twain's business affairs—chiefly the
typesetter and his publishing house—were in the saddle and riding him
hard. A cloud hung over his workshop, he complained, and the sense of
'fun' that had abounded when he began *A Connecticut Yankee* never
wholly returned. Not that the machine was without episodes of jubila-
tion for him. 'Saturday, January 5, 1889, 12:20 P.M.', Mark Twain wrote
in confident block letters in his notebook, 'I have seen a line of movable
type, *spaced and justified by machinery!* This is the first time in the
history of the world that this amazing thing has ever been done.' But
this 'immense historical birth', as he described the event for Orion, was
only the beginning of another, more expensive cycle of delays, breakdowns, tangled corporate and contractual arrangements. With the
exception of a brief period later in 1889, when it was used to set in galleys
the manuscript of Mark Twain's unfinished novel about Huck Finn and
Tom Sawyer out West among the Indians, the machine was disassembled.
Meanwhile, Mergenthaler's rival invention was proving its superiority
beyond any doubt.

In what proved to be a catastrophic gamble, Mark Twain risked his
entire stake in the venture upon his success in raising outside capital,

Opposite *The Rhône at Arles by Ed. Le Fevre. 'The main idea of the voyage was . . .
to rest up from sightseeing.'* Europe and Elsewhere

and in February 1891 the project collapsed. He had pinned his hopes on a consortium led by John Percival Jones, the millionaire Senator from Gold Hill, Nevada, who, during eight months in 1872, had watched the value of his shares in Virginia City's Crown Point Mine rocket from two dollars to eighteen hundred dollars. 'My capitalist', Clemens called him in February 1890; exactly a year later he was describing Jones to Joe Goodman as a fraud, 'a penny-worshipping humbug and shuffler', and 'really a very good sagebrush imitation of the Deity'. The Senator had backed out abruptly, explaining that he and other prudent men of substance in his consortium felt that conditions were not favorable for such a venture as the final development, manufacture, and marketing of Paige's wonderful machine; moreover, Jones added, somewhat inconsistently, a number of these men of substance already had large investments in Mergenthaler's Linotype. 'It is stupefying, it is unbelievable', Clemens said when he received the news. Several weeks later he told Orion, 'I've shook the machine and never wish to see it or hear it mentioned again.' He was horribly premature; it was to be years before he extricated himself, maimed and scarred for life, from his involvement in this venture, which he had believed (and until December 1894 continued to believe) would make him many times a millionaire.

Meanwhile, in 1891, determined to earn seventy-five thousand dollars in three months, he returned to writing for a living. Although his right hand was almost crippled with a sudden rheumatism, possibly hysterical in origin, he finished a new novel, a negligible farce called *The American Claimant*, which, in his depression he found altogether hilarious. Later in the year, when he was in Europe trying to grind out travel journalism and also taking the cure for his rheumatism at Aix-les-Bains (James Joyce's 'Aix-les-Pains'), he painfully taught himself to write with his left hand, and in his low mood all the symbolic meanings of doing something with one's left hand are relevant—'Nothing is so ignorant as a man's left hand', he was to say a few years later, 'except a lady's watch.' At the same time he made notes for a book which reflected his acceptance of defeat. Tom and Huck, both sixty years old in this projected but unwritten story, come back from their travels, mourn all the good things long gone, and agree that for each of them life has been a failure. 'They die together,' in Hannibal, where they had started. 'Tom and Huck die.'

The structure of Mark Twain's domestic life was crumbling along

Opposite *Terence V. Powderly, Grand Master Workman of the Knights of Labor, 1879–93. Lithograph by Kurz and Allison 1886*

with his morale as a writer. Livy entered a period of invalidism during which she suffered the onset of acute hyperthyroid heart disease. His daughters had grown to dread his 'sharp tongue and uncertain temper' and often preferred not to be left alone with him. Jean, the youngest, underwent an alarming change in personality; her ailment was soon to be diagnosed as epilepsy. On Susy—now a student at Bryn Mawr and so bitterly missed by her father that he was not sorry to hear she was home-sick—more than on the others, fell the burden of his worship, his accompanying demands for perfection, and his vulnerability to her slightest criticism.

With his creditors closing in on him, the house on Farmington Avenue, the warm and opulent center of his happiness at Nook Farm, had finally become impossible to keep up. He was going abroad now for an indefinite stay and as a matter of necessity. 'Travel has no longer any charms for me', he told Howells. 'I have seen all the foreign countries I want to see except heaven and hell, and I have only a vague curiosity as concerns one of those.' The Clemenses sailed for Europe in June 1891. They were gone for nearly nine years, and as a family they never lived in Hartford again.

That summer Clemens took a ten-day trip by raft down the Rhône to

Left Aix-les-Bains. 'I have seen all the foreign countries I want to except heaven and hell.' Letter to Howells, 1891. Right Bryn Mawr College in 1891: Susy Clemens and her classmates were harrowed by Mark Twain's ghost story, 'The Golden Arm'

Arles. But this symbolic return to the river of his earlier years, to a life of lazy comfort and 'extinction from the world', failed to replenish him, and the title of the book-length account he planned to write of the trip but never finished, *The Innocents Adrift*, characterizes his state of mind. He began *Pudd'nhead Wilson*, the dark novel in which he returned to Hannibal (moved down river below St Louis and renamed Dawson's Landing) and took his last long look at America, as a mistaken-identity farce about Siamese twins; it was only after a painful process of revision and 'a kind of literary Caesarean operation' that he managed to rescue the book.

In a different way he exploited the materials of Hannibal in *Tom Sawyer Abroad*; now Tom, Huck, and Jim travel about the world in a self-propelled balloon invented by a 'genius' who combines various primary traits of Pap Finn and James W. Paige. The story was heavily indebted to 'that French idiot', Jules Verne, just as its sequel, *Tom Sawyer, Detective*, was an attempt to cash in on the rage for Sherlock Holmes. And Mark Twain moved further back in time than 'boy life out on the Mississippi'. During 1893 he made plans for a magazine of news from 'the immemorial yesterdays of all time', and turning to the yesterday of Joan of Arc he began to write an unabashedly sentimental idealization of innocence and spirituality. *Personal Recollections of Joan of Arc*, whose heroine was partly modeled on Susy, was written out of love and 'not for lucre', he said, and it was to be his refuge from potboiling work, worry, and increasingly frustrating business trips to New York.

'It was wonderful to find America,' he was soon saying, as a sentiment for Columbus Day, 'but it would have been more wonderful to miss it.' Between June 1892 and May 1894 Clemens made four trips home, summoned from his family and his European seclusion by the rapidly worsening condition of his publishing house (now hopelessly over-extended and underfinanced) by 'gilt edge promises' which for a while revived his old faith in the typesetter, and by a general collapse of the economy. Before 1893 was out, five hundred banks and nearly sixteen thousand businesses had failed, the great railroads were in receivership, and soon, in the worst depression the country had yet experienced, two and a half million unemployed were to tramp the streets. In such 'hideous times' there was no hope for enterprises as shaky as Mark Twain's. 'This is simply a hell of a way to do business', he had grumbled impatiently in 1880. Now the heart's cry was different. 'Get me out of business, and I will be yours forever gratefully.' Livy agreed: 'I think Mr. Clemens is right in feeling that he should get out of business, that he is not fitted for it. It worries him too much.'

At a terrible low point in September 1893, when he felt 'the billows of

hell' rolling over him, he was rescued by 'the only man I care for in the world; the only man I would give a *damn* for'. This benefactor, five years younger than he, was Henry Huttleston Rogers, one of the architects, strategists, and managers of the Standard Oil trust, a financial freebooter celebrated for his personal charm and hospitality but chiefly for his daring, rapacity, and a seemingly total lack of business scruples. 'We are not in business for our health,' he had once said in a rare moment of public candor, 'but are out for the dollars.' His enemies called him 'Hell Hound' Rogers, compared him with rattlesnakes, sharks, and tigers, and thought of him as the victim of a 'cannibalistic money-hunger' which turned him into a 'fiend'. Even Samuel Clemens, who was to spend considerable time pondering the extent and meaning of his gratitude to this prince among robber barons, was willing to admit, 'He's a pirate all right, but he owns up to it and enjoys being a pirate. That's the reason I like him.'

Rogers was a poor boy who had made good and, unlike Mark Twain, made constantly better. Now, motivated by admiration, affection, and the shared experience of obscure beginnings, Rogers set about rescuing a great writer from probable destruction and the entire Clemens family from shame and relative want. 'You and I are a team,' Clemens was to say to Rogers gratefully; 'you are the most useful man I know, and I am the most ornamental.'

The early steps in his economic rehabilitation and eventual return to literature were agonizing. On Rogers's advice Clemens abandoned his publishing house, entered into voluntary bankruptcy proceedings on 18 April 1894, and then rejoined his family in Paris. At the end of the year Rogers told him that he must also abandon the last of his surviving expectations for the Paige typesetter. This advice, based on the disastrous results of a sixty-day test run in Chicago in competition with other typesetting machines, hit Clemens like a thunderclap, he told Rogers; he found himself wandering the streets of Paris 'with just barely head enough left on my shoulders to protect me from being used as a convenience by the dogs'.

It was only then, as Paige's marvelous machine took on its final

Opposite Above left *Henry Huttleston Rogers. 'A singularly clear-headed man.... And no grass grows under his feet.' Letter to Livy, 1893.* Above centre *26 Broadway, opposite Bowling Green: New York headquarters of the Standard Oil Company and Henry H. Rogers.* Above right *Sir Henry Irving. Like Bram Stoker (author of* Dracula*) the celebrated Shakespearian actor was an investor in Mark Twain's typesetter.* Below *Depression of 1893–4: Jacob Coxey's army of the unemployed marched from Massillon, Ohio to Washington*

Life's *Literary Side-Show, 1896*

aspect of a dissolved dream, that Clemens comprehended the full horror of his business failures and his bankruptcy. He had suffered not only a financial disaster which far exceeded anything his father had known in his bankruptcy, but also a failure of certain lifelong articles of belief. 'There's one thing which makes it difficult for me to soberly realize that my ten-year dream is actually dissolved', he told Rogers,

and that is, that it reverses my horoscope. The proverb says, 'Born lucky, *always* lucky,' and I am very superstitious. As a small boy I was notoriously lucky. It was usual for one or two of our lads (per annum) to get drowned in the Mississippi or in Bear Creek, but I was pulled out in a ⅔ drowned condition 9 times before I learned to swim, and was considered to be a cat in disguise. When the 'Pennsylvania' blew up and the telegraph reported my brother as fatally injured (with 60 others) but made no mention of me, my uncle said to my mother, 'It means that Sam was somewhere else, after being on that boat a year and a half—he was born lucky.' Yes, I *was* somewhere else. I am so superstitious that I have always been afraid to have business dealings with certain relatives and friends of mine because they were unlucky people. All my life I have stumbled upon lucky chances of large size, and whenever they were wasted it was because of my own stupidity and carelessness. And so I have felt entirely certain that that machine would turn up trumps eventually. It disappointed me lots of times, but I couldn't shake off the confidence of a life-time in my luck.

On 4 February 1894, on the silver anniversary of his marriage to Livy, he presented her, in love and remorse, with the symbol of his new circumstances, a silver five-franc piece. One hundred thousand dollars in debt, he was going to turn sixty that year; and, as he had heard, few men who failed in business at that age ever 'got up again'. The only way he could escape from his 'hellish dream', Rogers and Livy both told him, was to act contrary to all the conventional understandings of bankruptcy: following the pattern of another literary bankrupt, Sir Walter Scott, whom he despised, he was going to pledge himself publicly to paying off every penny of his debts. As his nephew, Samuel Moffett, of the San Francisco *Examiner*, trumpeted to the world, in this case 'honor knows no statute of limitations'. Having suffered the capitalist passion of bankruptcy, Mark Twain was now about to enjoy the capitalist resurrection. 'Our friend entered the fiery furnace a man', Andrew Carnegie was to say in tribute, 'and emerged a hero.'

Left *Rudyard Kipling. 'Between us we cover all knowledge. He knows all that can be known, and I know the rest.'* Right *Table Mountain, Cape Town harbor*

In July 1895 Clemens set out on a year-long round-the-world lecture tour that might have broken the stamina of someone younger but less determined. He began in high spirits. 'I shall arrive next January', he wrote to Rudyard Kipling about his imminent arrival in India,

> and you must be ready. I shall come riding my ayah with his tusks adorned with silver bells and ribbons and escorted by a troop of native howdahs richly clad and mounted upon a herd of wild bungalows; and you must be on hand with a few bottles of ghee, for I shall be thirsty.

He lectured his way across North America to Vancouver, then to Australia, New Zealand, Ceylon, India, and South Africa, and despite some black moments when he thought it useless 'to struggle against my ill luck any longer', he found himself considerably restored in morale and prosperity by his earnings and by the nearly unbroken ovation he received on his tour. From Cape Town in July 1896 he sailed for England, where he expected to spend six months or so writing a travel book, again for the benefit of his creditors, about his round-the-world tour. On 18 August 1896, in his rented house in the Surrey village of Guildford, just as he was thinking about nothing in particular, Clemens learned by cable that Susy, twenty-four, had died of meningitis in Hartford. 'It is one of the mysteries of our nature,' he reflected when nearly ten years had gone by since that black day, 'that a man, all unprepared, can receive a thunder-stroke like that and live.'

When Henry died on the river, Clemens was to tell Livy, he had not allowed himself to think of it, for fear that his grief would become too heavy; 'I have *hated* life before—from the time I was 18—but I was not indifferent to it', he said. But now he had no desire to put Susy out of his thoughts—he wanted to think about her death all the time, and he collected the precise circumstances of her death, her last words and acts, collected the scraps of writing that survived her final delirium and blindness. 'Mr. Clemens, Mr. Zola, Mr. Harte,' she had written, 'I see that even darkness can be great.' He cast about for someone to blame, and from time to time, irrationally, he settled on his nephew Charley Webster—'He was all dog . . . the primal cause of Susy's death and my ruin'—or on the Hartford neighbors who had nursed her and whose lack of wisdom and courage, he said, had permitted her 'wholly unnecessary death'. But mostly he blamed himself. He had spent sixty years, it seemed, hunting for a crime he could say he had committed—the tramp in the Hannibal-jail fire, Henry's death, the infant Langdon's death ('Yes, *I* killed him', he once told Howells). Even such a casual acquaintance as Mrs James T. Fields had noted that his whole life was 'one long apology'. Now his guilt crystallized so massively around the fact of Susy's death that his grief when Livy died eight years later was relatively restrained.

He invoked images drawn from his years in the East as writer and businessman. To describe his loss, he said, 'would bankrupt the vocabularies of all the languages to put it into words', and in the same way that 351 Farmington Avenue had symbolized and made tangible all the domestic bliss and opulence it was possible for a man to have, Susy's death had to be likened to a fire:

> A man's house burns down. The smoking wreckage represents only a ruined home that was dear through years of use and pleasant associations. By and by, as the days and weeks go by, he misses first this, then that, then the other thing. And when he casts about for it he finds that it was in that house. Always it is an *essential*—there was but one of its kind. It cannot be replaced. It was in that house. It is irrevocably lost. . . . It will be years before the tale of lost essentials is complete, and not till then can he truly know the magnitude of his disaster.

Susy Clemens, 1872–96

'My crimes made her a pauper and an exile', he said to Livy, who was herself in a 'submergence', he recognized. Livy sometimes sat solitary day after day wondering, without comfort, how it had all happened. 'We are a broken-hearted family,' she wrote to Mary Fairbanks, 'and such I think we must always remain.' She could no longer fall back on the religion of her girlhood, for he had long ago undermined this. As he later told his daughter Clara, he had violated the sanctities of Livy's 'spiritual shelter and refuge', and now she scarcely even believed in the immortality of the soul or in the existence of a just and purposeful deity instead of some sort of malign thug.

Guildford, Surrey

In Clemens's rented houses of mourning at Guildford and later in London, at Tedworth Square in Chelsea, Susy's sisters listened to their father rage against the vileness of life and the human race. He had been selfish and neglectful, he said, and he was sure that if she were to be brought back from the dead, he would still be selfish and neglectful, for he was condemned to obey the iron, brutish laws of his own nature and his race. 'It is an odious world, a horrible world', he was now given to saying. 'It is Hell; the true one.' But he also turned his grief and anger against himself, and what saved him was self-exploration, time and work.

'Wrote the first chapter of the book today', he noted on 24 October 1896. He had already decided that as soon as he finished *Following the Equator* he would begin on some other book, with no more than an hour between. 'I have many unwritten books to fly to for my preservation', he told Twichell. Livy reported: 'Mr. Clemens is going on with his work but he has found it very uphill work. . . . He goes to his study directly after breakfast and works until seven o'clock in the evening.' He was writing seven days each week and he intended to crowd thirty-one days into February. He revised *Following the Equator* at least three times, and Livy, too, as much for her benefit as for his, read his manuscript with unusual care. Her fifty-one pages of editorial notes, which he preserved among his papers, stressed clarity, accuracy, and fluency, but though they occasionally deal in matters of taste or delicacy, they fail to support the legend that her chief literary role in Mark Twain's life was that of prude.

'I am a mud image, and it puzzles me to know what is in me that writes', Clemens told Howells, 'and that has comedy fancies and finds pleasure in phrasing them.' He was writing a travel book 'whose outside aspect had to be cheerful, but whose secret substance was all made of bitterness and rebellion'. *Following the Equator* inevitably reflects the demoralizing circumstances of its composition, from its copyright caption in the name of Olivia L. Langdon (who, in the segregation of his assets in bankruptcy, had been declared a preferred creditor) to the rueful reflection on its last page, 'Human pride is not worthwhile; there is always something lying in wait to take the wind out of it.' Chapter 2 recounts the public episode in his life which had given him the most pride, his triumph at the Army of the Tennessee banquet in Chicago seventeen years earlier, and his association with General Grant; but as he sat in London at the end of April 1897 revising his manuscript, he had in mind a symbolic event then taking place in New York, the dedication of Grant's Tomb: '. . . the air is heavy with dirges and the boom of artillery'. In the sixth decade of Victoria's reign he had completed an equatorial tour of empire and imperialism, had seen the white man's secure dominion over alien races, black, brown, and yellow, and the accompanying victory of what he would soon be calling, as his indignation boiled to the surface, the 'Blessings-of-Civilization Trust'. In place of the gaiety and comedy fancies of some of Mark Twain's earlier travel writing, a certain note of protest and criticism is to be heard in *Following the Equator*, inconsistently (he writes with admiration of the British Raj in India) but in anticipation none the less of his public and private utterances of 1900–10.

Chapter Seven

The Dark Side of the Moon
1896–1900

In 1893, Frederick Jackson Turner, citing a recent census bulletin, pointed to the ending of a great historical movement: the frontiers of the Great West had closed. Mark Twain's own frontiers had also closed. His country was to go on to expansionist adventures beyond its continental limits. But in the early twilight of Mark Twain's life, having suffered frightful affronts to his frontier sense of plenitude and possibility, he felt frugality and defensiveness forced upon him, conservation, limits, self-inquiry, inwardness. The mood of 'carnival', in Erik Erikson's terms, had given way to the mood of 'atonement'.

In 1897 an American paper ran a headline five columns wide, 'Close of a Great Career', and under it the baseless story that Mark Twain, abandoned by his wife and daughters, was living in poverty. He raged in disgust after he read it. Only a man, he said, could be capable of such lying and vileness, not a dog or a cow. But, as he had told Rogers, he knew that his luck, which he had trusted all his life, had finally run out, and one day that winter he wrote out a list to prove it: the cook's sweetheart was dying, one of the maids might go blind, the porter had pleurisy, a friend's baby had died, another friend had fractured his skull, and on the way back from a visit to that friend in the hospital Clemens's cab had nearly run over a little boy in the street. 'Since bad luck struck us,' he concluded, 'it is risky for people to have to do with us.'

In order to reach an accommodation with the guilt and casualty that now seemed to be his daily bread, he began to write his 'Bible', a one-sided Socratic dialogue called *What Is Man?* He believed that all the

Opposite *Illustration by Gustave Doré for Poe's* The Raven

creeds giving dignity to God and man would crumble under the force of his angry determinist logic. 'We ignore and never mention the Sole Impulse which dictates and compels a man's every act,' he argued,

> the imperious necessity of securing his own approval, in every emergency and at all costs. To it we owe all that we are. It is our breath, our heart, our blood. It is our only spur, our whip, our goal, the only impelling power; we have no other. Without it we should be mere inert images, corpses; no one would do anything, there would be no progress, the world would stand still. We ought to stand reverently uncovered when the name of that stupendous power is uttered.

Tacitly invoking the Paige typesetter which had destroyed the structure of his life, he argued that the mind is a mere machine and that man, an automaton, 'is never anything but what his outside influences have made him' (or, as he was to say in another context, quoting a slave he had known in Hannibal. 'You tell me whar a man gits his corn pone, an' I'll tell you what his 'pinions is.' Throughout this runs an unacknowledged, contrary logic answering Mark Twain's deepest needs at this time: without choice there can be no responsibility, and without responsibility guilt has no meaning. 'No one', Bernard DeVoto wrote of *What Is Man?*, 'can read this wearisomely repeated argument without feeling the terrible force of an inner cry: "Do not blame me, for it was not my fault."' Livy loathed *What Is Man?* and would not permit her husband to read the last half to her. Out of consideration for her feelings Clemens did not publish it while she was alive, but its despairing ideas dominated his conversation. 'Pity is for the living, envy is for the dead', he wrote in *Following the Equator*—this was the mood his family came to dread.

At the same time as he was writing his 'Bible', Clemens followed another line of inquiry into guilt and responsibility. 'Everyone is a moon and has a dark side which he never shows to anybody', he wrote in his travel book, and now, living in mourning and seclusion, he turned inward to the enigmas of his life. 'S. L. C. interviews M. T.'—the idea recurs in the notebooks he kept during the late 1890s. He explored his dark side, found materials there more suggestive and more compelling than anything his conscious mind then presented to him, and in brief notes and outlines or in long, unfinished manuscripts he tried to elaborate a series of related fantasies into the form and dimension of fiction.

Like many other men living in an age when the speculative notion of an unconscious mind had become an intellectual commonplace, Clemens was fascinated by the psychically demonic, the ungovernable and con-

Opposite *Portrait by James Montgomery Flagg*

flictive in behavior. In 'The Facts Concerning the Recent Carnival of Crime in Connecticut', a paper he read to a Hartford discussion group in 1876, he investigated his own nagging sense of turmoil and multiplicity, an awareness that a number of identities, including those of Mr Clemens and Mark Twain, were clustered about a strangely guilty nucleus of personality called, for brevity's sake, 'S. L. C.'. He decided that every man had within him a demon and tyrant called 'conscience', whose function it is to whip him into guilt regardless of what a 'sound heart' might call right or wrong. 'Conscience' could be no more than the voice and code of society, as he was to dramatize in *Huckleberry Finn*, yet it generally ruled, and in his imagined 'carnival of crime' he vented the stored-up self-doubt, self-accusation, and anger which are the price of possessing 'conscience'.

Later, in Robert Louis Stevenson's *Dr. Jekyll and Mr. Hyde* (1886), he found a better explanation of the mystery of personality—'nearer, yes but not near enough', he said, for he recognized a falsity in Stevenson's scheme: unlike Jekyll and Hyde, 'the two persons in a man are wholly unknown to each other'. But in his sixty-first year, during the winter of 1896–7 in London, he found, he believed, the solution to what had become for him a haunting mystery.

He found the solution in a dream, which he recorded in his notebook:

I was suddenly in the presence of a negro wench who was sitting in grassy open country, with her left arm resting on the arm of one of those park-sofas that are made of broad slats with cracks between, and a curve-over back. She was very vivid to me—round black face, shiny black eyes, thick lips, very white regular teeth showing through her smile. She was about 22, and plump—not fleshy, not fat, merely rounded and plump; and good-natured and not at all bad-looking. She had but one garment on—a coarse tow-linen shirt that reached from her neck to her ankles without break. She sold me a pie; a mushy apple pie—hot. She was eating one herself with a tin teaspoon. She made a disgusting proposition to me. Although it was disgusting it did not surprise me—for I was young (I was never old in a dream yet) and it seemed quite natural that it should come from her. It was disgusting, but I did not say so; I merely made a chaffing remark, brushing aside the matter— a little jeeringly—and this embarrassed her and she made an awkward pretense that I had misunderstood her. I made a sarcastic remark about this pretense, and asked for a spoon to eat my pie with. She had but one, and she took it out of her mouth, in a quite matter-of-course way, and offered it to me.

Opposite *The drive to the Festspielhaus, Bayreuth, by G. Laska, 1890. 'Seven hours [of Parsifal] at five dollars a ticket is almost too much for the money.'* At the Shrine of St Wagner

My stomach rose—there everything vanished. . . . My, how vivid it all was! Even to the texture of her shirt, its dull white color, and the pale brown tint of a stain on the shoulder of it.

His solution to the 'haunting mystery' was to acknowledge the existence of a 'dream self' who comes alive during sleep, is liberated from normal restraints, and does things which the waking self would never dare even consider—in the dream which remained so vivid his other self had symbolically violated what was, for a 'young' Southerner, among the strictest because most alluring of sexual taboos.

'I go to unnameable places', Clemens wrote, in the excitement of his discovery, 'I do unprincipled things; and every vision is vivid, every sensation—physical as well as moral—is *real*.' Clemens's dream self lost his way in caves and in 'the corridors of monstrous hotels'. He

Left *'The man trampled calmly over the child's Body.' Illustration from Robert Louis Stevenson's* Dr Jekyll and Mr Hyde, *1886.* Right *Nightmare voyages: an encounter with a giant squid*

appeared at social gatherings dressed only in a nightshirt and told the people, 'I am Mark Twain'; no one believed him. He stood on the lecture platform and discovered that he had nothing at all to say; his audience began to leave, and after a while he found himself alone in the semi-darkness talking to an empty house. Sometimes he was standing at the wheel as his steamboat neared a black shadow, and he could not tell whether it was Selma Bluff, Hat Island, or a wall of night.

For a long time Clemens had been occupied with the blurred distinction between dream and reality. In 1893, with his disasters in business already looming in front of him, he wrote:

> I dreamed I was born & grew up & was a pilot on the Mississippi & a miner & a journalist in Nevada & a pilgrim in the *Quaker City* & had a wife & children & went to live in a villa at Florence—& this dream goes on & on & sometimes seems so real that I almost believe it is real. I wonder if it is? But there is no way to tell, for if one applies tests they would be part of the dream, too, & so would simply aid the deceit. I wish I knew whether it is a dream or real.

Once this confusion had been a subject for comedy. The Pauper was a bad dream that the Prince had, but with the Yankee, who is unable to wake from his dream and remains a stranger in the present, the comic possibilities vanished. Now, in the dark mood of Mark Twain's age and grief, the confusion has become nightmare.

For about two years after Susy died, Mark Twain explored a sort of deliberate, self-induced dream state in which the reality was what he dreamed and the fantasy what he lived by day, and he wrote stories about men whose bad dreams have become more real for them than waking reality. He traveled in the spectral world of Poe and Hawthorne, and among 'the invisible spheres' that Melville said 'were formed in fright'. 'When we remember that we are all mad,' Mark Twain said in his notebook, 'the mysteries of life disappear and life stands explained'; he exposed himself to madness, and for a while he was close enough to it to recognize that the dream, as Freud said, was simply 'a psychosis, with all the absurdities, delusions, and illusions of a psychosis.' Mark Twain's dream stories are characterized by dislocations of time, place, scale, and reality; such dislocations are frequently observed in psychotic or hallucinated states.

In general, these dream stories are of more relevance to the biographer and psychologist than they are to the critic and common reader. For while they fail as fiction they deal, often in specific autobiographical terms, with the issues of guilt and responsibility, with the experience of the destruction of identity and the sudden, numbing recognition of the possibility of having no 'real' existence whatsoever. Mark Twain's life takes on a terrifying coherence in these stories: a man rises to eminence, lives on a plateau of triumph, happiness, and fulfillment, and then his luck runs out—he 'dreams' or 'lives' a life of disgrace and horror. When he 'wakes' from his dream his hair has turned white and he is crazed, incapable of knowing which of his existences he should believe in.

In one of these stories the narrator, reduced to microscopic size, goes on a terrifying voyage within a drop of water. In another he has become a cholera organism inhabiting the bloodstream of a tramp whose stomach is 'the mighty Republic of Getrichquick . . . the greatest of the democracies'. The businessman's dream of wealth has become the writer's and the moralist's nightmare, and even in the most remote settings Mark Twain comes back to the subject of money—real money, counterfeit money, forged checks, and useless money, as in a story about sailors marooned for life on an uncharted island but having in their possession fifteen million dollars in gold.

According to John S. Tuckey, who, in his editing of *Which Was the Dream?* (1967), has imposed on a once baffling mass of 'symbolic writings' an authoritative chronological and thematic order, Mark Twain worked at this body of fiction like a man pursued by furies; he turned out manuscript after manuscript, often with no thought of publication. It hardly seems possible, said Bernard DeVoto, the first to recognize the role of these manuscripts in Mark Twain's ordeal, that any man could write so much. There are no masterpieces here, no near-masterpieces, but instead a lot of defeat and false starts, poignant evidences of a man on the edge of nullity and saving himself through work. He survived his ordeal, and that, considering what he had gone through, is in itself something of a triumph. It illuminates with a grim retrospective irony the celebrated public statement that Mark Twain made in June 1897— less than a month after he began writing *Which Was the Dream?*—to the London correspondent of the New York *Journal*: 'The report of my death was an exaggeration.'

What he had learned about the workings of the dream mind had carried him as far as he could go toward exonerating himself. Eventually he favored *What Is Man?* as gospel for 'the damned human race' and turned to a philosophical nihilism which enabled him to blur the distinction between the real world and the dream world, or, using other familiar co-ordinates, between truth and lies. '*Nothing* exists', Satan declares in the chapter which now concludes *The Mysterious Stranger*:

Strange, indeed, that you should not have suspected that your universe and its contents were only dreams, visions, fiction! Strange, because they are so frankly and hysterically insane—like all dreams. . . . There is no God, no

London, 1896–7. Photographer's proofs selected by Mark Twain

universe, no human race, no earthly life, no heaven, no hell. It is all a dream
—a grotesque and foolish dream. Nothing exists but you. And you are but a
thought—a vagrant thought, a useless thought, a homeless thought, wandering forlorn among the empty eternities!

Mark Twain had begun his career as a teller of tall stories, a hoaxer,
a humorist; and in the despairing (and broken) logic of *A Mysterious
Stranger* humor alone promises some sort of temporary salvation:

Your race, in its poverty, has unquestionably one really effective weapon—
laughter. Power, money, persuasion, supplication, persecution—these can
lift at a colossal humbug—push it a little—weaken it a little, century by
century; but only laughter can blow it to rags and atoms at a blast. Against
the assault of laughter nothing can stand. You are always fussing and
fighting with your other weapons. Do you ever use that one?

As his vision matured, writing became a delicately controlled illusion in which the 'truth', in order to be accepted, often had to be dis-

The trial of Captain Dreyfus. A 'silent colossal National Lie'

guised as a lie. 'I disseminate my true views', Mark Twain was to tell an interviewer in 1900, 'by means of a series of apparently humorous and mendacious stories', and, as he became a fully engaged critic of society, he was willing to argue with some passion that all spoken lies put together existed in a proportion of '1 to 22,894' to 'the silent colossal National Lie' that had supported such tyrannies and shams as slavery and the conviction of Captain Dreyfus. But at some point in this development, fiction, dreams, and lies had become interchangeable—they were all 'frankly and hysterically insane'.

The fiction Mark Twain wrote after his ordeal no longer has the rich sprawl of accident and anecdote of his work of the 1870s and 1880s. Instead it is frequently marked by spareness in structure and invention and by moral and logical clarity. The best of this fiction—*The Man that Corrupted Hadleyburg*, for example—has a crystalline sardonic power; the worst of it—stories such as 'A Horse's Tale'—is merely sentimental.

In addition to quasi-philosophic tales, Mark Twain was to be most at home in reminiscence, polemic, and protest, and to bring himself to write or dictate he relied for stimulus on larger and larger doses of indignation derived from and redirected toward Mary Baker Eddy, King Leopold II of Belgium, William Shakespeare, God, and a considerable range of social, political, and economic injustices.

During Clemens's rise, fall, and early rehabilitation, Orion, with a minimum of complaint, had followed an unvarying pattern of vicissitude and decline. Along with a number of other inventions, Orion had given up the grand scheme of his life, a flying machine; as a writer he had no readers, as a lawyer no clients; a lecture he gave in Keokuk, 'Man, the Architect of Our Religion', got him excommunicated by the church elders. Various schemes to cash in on the Tennessee land had failed; so had a chicken farm he started with a loan from Sam. He and his wife,

Orion and Mollie Clemens

Mollie, ended up keeping a boardinghouse in Keokuk, and on 30 November 1897, when he wrote to congratulate Sam on his sixty-second birthday, Orion was at work on a new literary scheme, a book which would penetrate the mystery of the Essene sect known as the Society of the Dead Sea. He was also proposing himself as model for a 'fool character' in a comic novel he wanted Sam to write. Eleven days after this letter Orion was dead. 'He was good—all good and sound: there was nothing bad in him, nothing base, nor any unkindness', Sam wrote to Mollie from Vienna. 'It was unjust that such a man, against whom no offense could be charged, should have been sentenced to live for 72 years.'

Soon after the death of Orion—Sam's mirror image, cautionary brother, baseline for judging the distance he had traveled from Hannibal—the tide of Clemens's affairs began to turn. 'I hear that your latest work is succeeding splendidly,' Howells wrote from New York in January 1898, 'and I have lately heard people talking proudly and gladly of your rehabilitation in the business line.' *Following the Equator* had sold thirty thousand copies right away; the royalties and the earnings from various investments Rogers had made for Clemens added up, by the end of that January, to enough to pay off the creditors in full and still leave thirteen thousand to spare. 'The debts . . . took the *spirit out of my work*', Clemens had told Rogers in December, 1897. 'For the first time in my life I am getting more pleasure out of paying money than pulling it in.' He began to feel 'abundant peace of mind' once again, and Livy, too, showed signs of coming out of her depression. Rogers had sent on the letters of thanks and acknowledgment from the satisfied creditors, and Livy, reading them over and over again, told Clemens that this was the first happy day she had had since Susy died. Within the next two years a substantial measure of the old prosperity returned to him along with his chronic hunger (this time kept reasonably in check) for sure things that would make him millions: a weaving machine that reproduced photographic images and promised to make him the Carnegie of carpets; a granulated high-protein food concentrate called Plasmon which offered cheap nutrition and a cure for heartburn.

Clemens's notebook entries became a sort of antiphony of dream stories and records of his rising cash balances. Between October 1898 and April 1899 his account with Rogers increased from $18,068.89 to $51,995.29. In January 1899 'a quite unexpected $10,000 tumbled in here,' he joyously told Howells. 'Come—respect the capitalist!' Cables

Opposite *Door of Dreams by Georges de Feure, 1897–8.* Overleaf *Vienna: The Ringstrasse at Night by Maximilian Lenz, 1898*

between Rogers and Clemens now told a new story. 'Profit $16,000', Rogers reported after closing out a stock investment. 'Splendid bird', Clemens replied. 'Set her again', and he watched the swelling of his 'hen-fruit': Federal Steel up in two weeks from thirty-two to thirty-eight and a half, Brooklyn Gas up from seventy-five to one hundred and fifty-five. He was feeling young and comfortable again, free of the long nightmare of leaving his family in want, invigorated, too, in health and morale by his discovery of a cure for the physical ills of the human race, Osteopathy, then also known as 'the Swedish movements'.

Livy, keeper of the accounts and the bankbook, figured up with pencil and paper for her own satisfaction that they owned a house and furniture in Hartford, that his royalties in America and England were equivalent to the income from an invested capital of two hundred thousand dollars, and that they had one hundred and seven thousand dollars cash in the bank. 'I have been out and bought a box of 6-cent cigars; I was smoking $4\frac{1}{2}$ before', he told Howells after this accounting in January 1899, and he said that they were thinking of coming back to New York to live next year. Meanwhile, in Vienna, they were living in *de luxe* hotels, in enormous suites of four bedrooms, a dining room, drawing room, three bathrooms, and three antechambers, and were treated like Habsburgs. 'For God's sake, let him pass,' said a mounted officer ordering a police barrier opened. 'Don't you see it's Herr Mark Twain?' 'My,' Clemens said to Clara after they had passed through, 'but that makes me feel damned good.'

He and Livy had begun to come out of seclusion. Afternoons, from five o'clock on, a stream of visitors poured into their drawing room, which was becoming a sort of second American Embassy. He felt that during his nearly ten years of self-exile he had been serving as 'self-appointed Ambassador at Large of the U. S. of America—without salary'. And from America itself were coming unmistakable evidences that during this time of his low creativity and morale his reputation had passed through a remarkable change. Popularity had turned into fame. He had become a part of his nation's history as well as a standard author whose works were now being published in a signed and numbered twenty-two-volume edition. The biographical sketch for this edition, written by Clemens's nephew Sam Moffett but drafted by Clemens himself, invoked the dialectic movement of Mark Twain's life between Hannibal and the great world. The sketch concludes with a discussion of Mark Twain as 'characteristically American in every fiber', yet possessing a 'universal

Opposite *Old Battersea Bridge: Nocturne, Blue and Gold, by James A. McNeill Whistler*

At Dollis Hill House, London, 1900

quality' which has made him 'a classic, not only at home, but in all lands
whose people read and think about the common joys and sorrows of
humanity'.

In 1884 the *Critic* had asked its readers to nominate forty American
'immortals'. Holmes, Lowell, and Whittier led the list, Howells was fifth,
Bret Harte eighth, and Mark Twain fourteenth, one place ahead of
Charles Dudley Warner and two places ahead of Henry Ward Beecher.
In 1899 John Kendrick Bangs, editor of the American edition of the trans-
atlantic journal *Literature*, asked his readers to nominate ten living
writers for a hypothetical American Academy. Howells was first with
eighty-four votes, the popular philosopher and historian John Fiske
was second with eighty-two, and Mark Twain was third with eighty.
'Your 84 votes place you where you belong—at the head of the gang',
Clemens wrote from Vienna. But the readers of *Literature* had already

been told by Howells in June 1898 that the greatest American literary center was at present neither in New York nor in Boston but in Vienna, and from Howells directly Clemens had received a string of heartfelt tributes compounded of love, admiration, and Howells's unswerving conviction that, polls and academies and other literary men aside, his friend was 'sole, incomparable, the Lincoln of our literature'. 'I wish you could understand how unshaken you are, you old tower, in every way', Howells wrote in January 1898. 'Your foundations are struck so deep that you will catch the sunshine of immortal years and bask in the same light as Cervantes and Shakespeare.' And that October, after rereading 'The Recent Carnival of Crime', he concluded, 'You are the greatest man of your sort that ever lived, and there is no use saying anything else.'

His life had become history and biography, legend and stereotype, expressing the values and achievements of his country and his century. His rise from obscurity and poverty, his triumphs, his bankruptcy, and then his recovery of financial honor—these had made him a hero of the American experience, and when he came home in 1900 he was given a hero's welcome and led a hero's public life. Meanwhile, living out in London his last year of 'everlasting exile', Clemens looked back on history, and against the perspective of time his bitterness faded momentarily and he remembered only the fulfillments. 'The 20th Century is a stranger to me', he wrote in his notebook. 'I wish it well, but my heart is all for my own century. I took 65 years of it, just on a risk, but if I had known as much about it as I know now I would have taken the whole of it.'

Chapter Eight

'The most conspicuous person on the planet'
1900–10

'I come back from my exile young again, fresh and alive, and ready to begin life once more', Clemens said in November 1900 at a New York dinner in his honor. Vigorous, playful, and smiling as he stepped off the gangplank of the steamship *Minnehaha* ('Laughing Water', as readers of *Hiawatha* knew), he had come home to an ovation that was to go on for the rest of his life. Newspapers all over the country hailed the return of 'the bravest author in all literature' and followed the lead of the *New York Times* in paying tribute to 'the Hero as Man of Letters' and to a national morality solidly based on commercial honor. 'It is a great thing to possess genius,' the Boston *Weekly Transcript* said; 'it is a greater thing to be a man of unsullied honor.' Mark Twain was as funny as ever, one reporter noted, but a little better-natured than he used to be. Now, instead of dodging interviewers, he freely discussed with the press his belief that 'the trouble with us in America is that we haven't learned to speak the truth', and he outlined his short-range plans to spend the winter in New York (which he conceded was 'cleaner than Bombay'), to work and travel as little as possible, and to run for President on the broad platform of being in favor of everything.

Settled in at a furnished house on West Tenth Street, he received a stream of visitors who solicited his opinions on heaven and hell, the Boer War and the Boxer Rebellion, and his favorite method of escaping from the Indians. 'It always puzzled me', his daughter Clara recalled, 'how Mark Twain could manage to have an opinion on every incident, accident, invention, or disease in the world.' He set out on a round of

Opposite *On Fifth Avenue*

Delmonico's, Fifth Avenue at 44th Street, New York

lunches, club banquets, speeches, and public appearances that at first nearly devoured him and left him exhausted after the almost nightly 'dreadful ordeal' of dinner music, clashing cutlery, and shrieking human voices rising in competition with one another toward sheer pandemonium. Howells commented, 'I hate to see him eating so many dinners and writing so few books.' Yet the sufficient reward of these occasions for Mark Twain was love, homage, and the moment when he rose to speak and give play to his spellbinding presence and personality.

'The most satisfying and spirit-exalting honor done me in all my seventy years, oh, by seventy times seventy!' he was to say of the birthday celebration at Delmonico's on 5 December 1905. There, against a background of potted palms, gilt mirrors, and the music of a forty-piece orchestra from the Metropolitan Opera House, Colonel George Harvey, president of Harper and Brothers, had assembled what was in effect a living tableau of Mark Twain's years in the East: writers like Howells and Cable; old friends like Twichell; the plutocrats Rogers and Andrew Carnegie; editors, critics, humorists; respectable, workaday literary practitioners who would soon be forgotten but were now the night sky for the brilliance of Mark Twain's departing comet. In his funny and sad speech, neither the first nor the last of his series of swan songs, he looked back over the seventy years since his birth in 'a little hamlet, in the backwoods of Missouri, where nothing ever happened', and he joked about his morals ('an acquirement—like music, like a foreign language, like piety, poker, paralysis') and his habits. 'It has always been my rule never to smoke when asleep, and never to refrain when awake', he said, but confessed, 'I have stopped smoking now and then, for a few months at a time, but it was not on principle, it was only to show off; it was to pulverize those critics who said I was a slave to my habits and couldn't break my bonds.' The lesson of all this was, 'We can't reach old age by another man's road. My habits protect my life, but they would assassinate you.' Having reached 'Pier Number Seventy', he was prepared, he told his hearers—and he believed it himself for the moment—to sail again 'toward the sinking sun' with 'a reconciled spirit' and 'a contented heart'.

On the streets and in theatres and restaurants Mark Twain was so often pointed out and applauded that, as Clara said, 'it was difficult to realize he was only a man of letters'. He had, in fact, become something more—sage, oversoul, spokesman, and a hero of a distinctly antiheroic and vernacular sort. His career had followed a mythic pattern of journey from obscurity and poverty in Hannibal, mortal struggle, victory, and return. His fame had also been affected by a series of revolutions in the printing and distribution of news and in the public appetite for news. He became, without parallel or equal, a celebrity—in Daniel Boorstin's definition, 'a person who is known for his well-knownness'. He was to be the subject of countless news stories which, by the dynamics of celebrity and through his own brilliant management, made him even better copy and brought him closer to realizing his declared ambition to be the 'most conspicuous person on the planet'. And he may actually have realized this ambition in June 1907, when he journeyed to England (he would have been even willing 'to journey to Mars', he said) to receive the degree of Doctor of Literature from Oxford and the robe of scarlet and gray which he cherished and flaunted from then on.

The reporters who dogged his steps wherever he went were attracted not so much by his literature as by his vividness and his genius for generating news and 'effects' (like his Connecticut Yankee), his astonishing opinions and mannerisms, his mane of white hair which he washed with soap each morning, and the white suits that he took to wearing after 1906. That December, standing up to testify before a joint committee on copyright in Washington, he stripped off his long overcoat. Dressed from shoulder to foot in white serge, he was like a blaze of sunlight in the dimly lighted room at the Library of Congress. Then, as he had been doing for years, he spoke out, like Charles Dickens, in defense of intellectual property rights and in anticipation of the happy day when, as he had said long before, 'in the eyes of the law, literary property will be as sacred as whiskey, or any other of the necessaries of life.'

His dazzling white outfits made him, he claimed, 'absolutely the only cleanly clothed human being in all Christendom north of the Tropics'. But in their assertion of an inner purity as well (Howells called him 'whited sepulchre') the famous white suits answered to a lifetime hunger for love and expiation. White was the garb of publicness for Mark Twain, just as it had been the garb of reclusiveness for Emily Dickinson. Dressed in white he would walk up Fifth Avenue to Fifty-ninth Street on a Sunday morning and rest in the lobby of the Plaza Hotel until the churches were out; then he walked homeward along sidewalks crowded with fashionable strangers who lifted their hats to him in recognition and homage. 'It was his final harvest,' said his biographer, who accompanied him on these walks, 'and he had the courage to claim it.'

Largely through Rogers's management and advice, Clemens was once again a man of wealth and property who was associated with a succession of edifices as imposing in their way as the Hartford house, which he sold at a loss in 1903: a mansion on the Hudson, at Riverdale, New York; a fifty-thousand-dollar house in Tarrytown which he bought but never lived in; a villa on the outskirts of Florence; the building at 21 Fifth Avenue, on the corner of Ninth Street; and finally 'Stormfield', an Italianate villa which, with earnings from his serialized autobiography, he built on a hilltop at Redding, Connecticut. In October 1903 Rogers negotiated for him a contract with Harper and Brothers which guaranteed him a minimum of twenty-five thousand dollars a year for the next five years, and Clemens could afford to pick and choose among a variety of attractive offers and reject most of them, including a lecture tour at one thousand dollars a night. As the years went on, Clemens was often to be seen in the company of various plutocrats at Palm Beach, Bermuda, Tuxedo Park. His friendship with Rogers had continued to deepen—'I am his principal intimate, and that is my idea of him.' Stretched out on the sofa in Rogers's private office in the Standard Oil Building at 26 Broadway, smoking or reading while Rogers conducted his daily affairs, Clemens appeared to be completely at home and completely untroubled, even at a time when each new issue of *McClure's* and other muckraking magazines presented harrowing evidence of the menace of Standard Oil in particular and big business in general. At

Opposite Above left *June 1907. On board S.S.* Minneapolis, *bound for England.* Above centre *In white. 'I prefer to be clean in the matter of raiment—clean in a dirty world.'* Above right *London: Savage Club dinner in his honor.* Below *Lobby and Palm Court, Plaza Hotel, New York*

SAVAGE CLUB
HOUSE DINNER

JULY 6TH
19—

MENU

Soup
Mock Turtle

Fish
Turbot
Sauce Hollandaise

Removes
Hind Quarter of Lamb
Mint Sauce
Roast Duckling
& Green Peas

Sweets
Fruit Jellies
Charlotte á la Russe

Savoury
Soft Roes on Toast

Mark Twain

Sir James D. Linton
in the Chair

WELCOME TO
MARK TWAIN

home, almost every day and night for the rest of his life, Clemens played billiards, 'the best game on earth', on a table given him as a Christmas present by Mrs Rogers. He had also become Andrew Carnegie's crony and dinner companion, the recipient not only of Carnegie's numbing brand of commercial wisdom—'Put all your eggs into one basket, and watch that basket'—but also of bottles, cases, and finally barrels of Carnegie's private-stock Scotch—'the best and the smoothest whisky now on the planet'. It had become almost as fitting to identify Mark Twain with the motorcar and the steam yacht, symbols of the plutocracy (along with the silk hat he sometimes wore), as with the stagecoach and river boat by which he had traveled away from Hannibal's Hill Street toward Fifth Avenue.

For Mark Twain, who all his life dreamed of being rich but at the same time believed that money was evil and fostered evil, there had to be some price for his alliance with the plutocracy, and this price was a sporadic blunting and demoralizing of purpose, a reinforcement of his belief that what made the world turn was self-interest, conformity, and hunger for approval. As a businessman and provisional plutocrat, he embraced business values, but as writer, critic, and moralist, he rejected them and cast a savage eye upon American society. 'Money lust has always existed,' he told Twichell, 'but not in the history of the world was it ever a craze, a madness, until your time and mine.'

> Like all the other nations, we worship money and the possessors of it—they being our aristocracy, and we have to have one. We like to read about rich people in the papers; the papers know it, and they do their best to keep this appetite liberally fed. They even leave out a football game or a bull fight now and then in order to get room for all the particulars of how—according to the display heading—'Rich Woman Fell Down Cellar—Not Hurt.' The falling down the cellar is of no interest to us when the woman is not rich; but no rich woman can fall down a cellar and we not yearn to know all about it and wish it was us.

He was as certain that America was headed toward a plutocracy or monarchy as he was that Christian Science was the coming religion. 'When we contemplate her and what she has achieved,' he said about Mary Baker Eddy, 'it is blasphemy to longer deny to the Supreme Being the possession of a sense of humor.' In a series of articles published during 1902 and 1903 (and, with much new material, as a book in 1907),

Opposite Above left *Riverdale-on-Hudson, New York, 1901–3*. Above centre *Tuxedo Park, New York, summer 1907*. Above right *'Stormfield', Redding, Connecticut, 1908–10*. Below *Emblems of the plutocracy: out for a ride, 21 May 1907*

he went at Eddyism with the same merciless logic with which he had catalogued 'Fenimore Cooper's Literary Offenses' during the 1890s. Cooper's *Deerslayer*, he had said, 'is just simply a literary delirium tremens'—its author saw 'as through a glass eye, darkly'. But Mrs Eddy had such a clear sight of human weakness and need that a 'colossal future' lay ahead for her 'cult': 'I am selling my Lourdes stock and buying Christian Science trust. I regard it as the Standard Oil of the future.'

'The political and commercial morals of the United States are not merely food for laughter,' he declared in an autobiographical dictation, 'they are an entire banquet.' He could speak as a seasoned victim as well as an observer. The 'strange panic' of October 1907 made him think of 'a mighty machine which has slipped its belt'. A chief casualty in the panic was the Knickerbocker Trust Company of New York where ('just my God-damned luck!') he had fifty-one thousand dollars on deposit, his 'autobiography money', he called it, for it freed him from other work. His sentiment for Thanksgiving that year was pure gratitude. 'I am thankful—thankful beyond words—that I had only fifty-one thousand dollars on deposit in the Knickerbocker Trust, instead of a million; for if I had had a million in that bucket shop, I should be nineteen times as sorry as I am now.' He wondered just how many other Knickerbocker

Left *Andrew Carnegie's simplified spelling was 'all right enough', Mark Twain said at a 1907 banquet, 'but, like chastity, you can carry it too far'. Sketch by Césare.* Right *Mary Baker Eddy. Christian Science was 'the Standard Oil of the future'*

depositors found as little solace as he did in the motto, 'In God we trust.'

That December he had a talk with Carnegie about an intriguing story to the effect that Theodore Roosevelt—'the Tom Sawyer of the political world of the twentieth century', Clemens called him—had precipitously decided to abolish the motto 'In God we trust', because 'coins carried the name of God into improper places'. The fact was, Carnegie said, that 'the name of God is used to being carried into improper places everywhere and all the time'. It *was* a beautiful motto, Clemens said. 'It is simple, direct, gracefully phrased; it always sounds well—In God we trust. I don't believe it would sound any better if it were true.' But the fact was, he went on, it hadn't been true since the Civil War; what the country trusted in was not God but 'the Republican party and the dollar —mainly the dollar'. And as for the United States being a Christian country (as twenty-two clergymen, protesting Roosevelt's order, had just declared in a formal resolution), 'Why, Carnegie,' Clemens said, and one can hear the triumphant drawl, the soft and deadly pounce, 'so is hell.'

He also took a savage delight in Carnegie's own egotistic gambols ('He has bought fame,' he said of Carnegie's celebrated public libraries which all bore his name, 'and paid cash for it'), in John D. Rockefeller Jr's avocation as Sunday-school teacher, and even in a discomfiture of the Standard Oil Company. When Judge Kenesaw Mountain Landis fined Standard Oil of Indiana a total of nearly twenty-nine and a quarter million dollars for taking rebates in violation of the Elkins Act, Clemens said he was reminded of what the bride said after her wedding night— 'I expected it but didn't suppose it would be so big.'

But this sort of hilarity Clemens tended to keep as private as those diatribes against money, money men, and money morality which he spoke as from beyond the grave, intending them only for his posthumous autobiography. 'Only dead men can tell the truth in this world', he said, implicitly defining his need to put his most deeply felt opinions—subversive opinions which attacked the premises of society and conventional belief—in the mouths of dead men or of mysterious strangers and social outcasts: Satan; the 'passing stranger' who returned to Hadleyburg to corrupt the town; Jerry, the 'gay and impudent and satirical and delightful young black man' of Hannibal, who preached secular sermons from the top of his master's woodpile and pronounced the searing text, 'You tell me whar a man gits his corn pone, an' I'll tell you what his 'pinions is.' When Livy fell ill in 1902 Clemens explained to his publisher, 'I have no editor—no censor', but after she died in 1904 it was to become uncomfortably clear that during all these years of his existence as a 'suppressed writer', when he had put the blame on Livy, his severest censor had in reality been himself. 'We write frankly and fearlessly,' he said years earlier, 'but then we "modify" before we print.'

Luxuriating in his celebrity, he recognized that celebrity had its costs and imperatives and that it was not a permanency at all, but instead the frail child of public opinion. 'We all do no end of feeling and we mistake it for thinking,' he wrote in 1900, developing Jerry's text in 'Corn-Pone Opinions'. 'And out of it we get an aggregation which we consider a boon. Its name is Public Opinion. It is held in reverence. It settles everything. Some think it is the Voice of God.' He put this bitter essay away in what he had taken to calling his box of 'posthumous stuff'. But he remembered its lesson well and allowed it to shape many of his actions. His response to bankruptcy, bereavement, and a sense of failing powers—as traumatic an experience for him as the blacking factory had been for Charles Dickens—was, on occasion, a refusal to take serious risks, in public, with what he had regained.

Horrified and shamed by lynchings in the South and even in Missouri during 1901 and 1902, Clemens wrote a magazine article which he intended as an introduction to a history of lynching. 'O kind missionary, O compassionate missionary,' he wrote, 'leave China! come home and convert these Christians!' But instead of sending 'The United States of Lyncherdom' off to the *North American Review* he consigned it to his pile of posthumous manuscripts, and he abandoned the book altogether. For he had realized that what was at stake was not only his book sales in the South but something as precious to him as his sense of right, the ties to his homeland. 'I shouldn't have even half a friend left down there, after it issued from the press,' he reasoned.

Desouthernized as he was, his imagination and his youth still dwelled down there, in Hannibal, 'a great and beautiful country', he was to say on his sixty-seventh birthday, 'a delectable land' with 'the most enchanting river view the planet could furnish'. He was intermittently occupied with new Tom and Huck stories in which the boys, old and withered, come back and meet after fifty years. He himself came back to Hannibal in May 1902 for what was to be the last time, visited the house on Hill Street, and, choked with emotion, accepted the love and applause of the townspeople. Along the way to Columbia, Missouri, where the university made him a doctor of laws, other crowds waited for him with applause and flowers, and his eyes filled with tears. For the sake of this love for his homeland he had put away his article on lynching and had

Opposite *With Livy, New York, 1900 or 1901*

reasoned, self-consolingly, 'There is plenty of vitriol in it and that will keep it from spoiling.'

'I am a revolutionist—by birth, breeding, principle, and everything else,' Clemens told reporters in April 1906 and then explained why, none the less, he had had to disassociate himself from Maxim Gorky, who had come to America to raise money for the overthrow of the Czar. Gorky's 'efficiency as a persuader', Clemens said, had become seriously 'impaired'—'I was about to say destroyed'—because he had violated American codes of conduct: Gorky, as the press and public had just learned, was traveling with a woman who was not his wife. 'The man might just as well have appeared in public in his shirttail,' Clemens said. (On a happier occasion he had once observed that 'naked people have little or no influence in society'.) Gorky had violated custom, and according to Clemens's pragmatic reasoning, this was worse than violating the law—law is only sand, he said, but 'custom is custom; it is built of brass, boiler iron, granite; facts, reasonings, arguments have no more effect upon it than the idle winds have upon Gibraltar'. By such facts, reasonings, arguments, Clemens attempted to dissipate the mortification of his own considered retreat before 'Public Opinion', which 'settles everything'. For it was surely mortifying for a 'revolutionist' to withdraw his support from a hundred and fifty million Russians in their revolution just because one of them left his trousers at home.

Suppressions and *démarches* aside, much of the intended social criticism of Mark Twain's last ten years remains as pertinent now as it was for the generation of the muckrakers. When he started on his round-the-world tour in 1895, as he later told an interviewer, he had been 'a red-hot imperialist. I wanted the American eagle to go screaming into the Pacific. It seemed tiresome and tame for it to content itself with the Rockies.' The Spanish-American War (which Howells predicted would inaugurate 'an era of blood-bought prosperity') impressed Clemens at first as 'a righteous war', the only occasion in history when one nation had been willing to fight for another's freedom. He may even have believed, as he said in November 1900, that 'the Yellow Terror is threatening this world today. It is looming vast and ominous.' But soon the application of American force to the 'liberation' of the Philippines fused in his mind with the lessons of the Boer War and the Boxer reparations. In December 1900, when he introduced the twenty-six-year-old Winston Churchill to his first American lecture audience, Clemens said, 'I think that England sinned when she got herself into a

Opposite Andrew Carnegie by Anders Zorn. 'He has bought fame and paid cash for it.' Overleaf Central Park, New York, by Maurice Prendergast, 1901

Maurice B. Prendergast

war in South Africa, just as we have sinned in getting into a similar war in the Philippines.' And for the New York *Herald* on 30 December he supplied a bitter salute to the twentieth century:

> I bring you the stately matron named Christendom, returning bedraggled, besmirched, and dishonored from pirate raids in Kiao-Chou, Manchuria, South Africa, and the Philippines, with her soul full of meanness, her pocket full of boodle, and her mouth full of pious hypocrisies. Give her soap and a towel, but hide the looking-glass.

In the *North American Review* of February 1901 he published 'To the Person Sitting in Darkness', an attack on the 'Blessings-of-Civilization Trust', its managers (Mr McKinley, Mr Joseph Chamberlain, the Kaiser, and the Czar), and its chosen representatives, the Christian missionaries who marched to distant lands to conquer under the double sign of the cross and the black flag. He pressed the attack in a second article, 'To My Missionary Critics'. 'Praise be to the Eternal!' said a leading anti-imperialist. 'A voice has been found.' A few years later his target became the Belgian depredations in the Congo, and he wrote 'King Leopold's Soliloquy', the most effective and most widely circulated piece of American propaganda in the cause of Congo reform.* After his death it became clear from two posthumous publications, 'The War Prayer' and *The Mysterious Stranger*, that Mark Twain had gone far beyond anti-imperialism. He indicted the martial spirit in general together with the hysteria and brutalization that he said inevitably accompanied it. 'I can see a million years ahead', Satan says in a remarkable passage from *The Mysterious Stranger*:

> The loud little handful—as usual—will shout for the war. The pulpit will—warily and cautiously—object—at first; the great, big, dull bulk of the nation will rub its sleepy eyes and try to make out why there should be a war, and will say, earnestly and indignantly, 'It is unjust and dishonorable, and there is no necessity for it.' Then the handful will shout louder. A few fair men on the other side will argue and reason against the war with speech and pen, and at first will have a hearing and be applauded; but it will not last long; those others will outshout them, and presently the antiwar audiences will thin out and lose popularity. Before long you will see this curious thing: the

* His moral passion did not blind Mark Twain to the force of 'Public Opinion' and the wisdom of the market place. He shared his publishers' feelings that it was not altogether prudent, commercially, for him to have dipped into Leopold's 'stinkpot,' or Mrs Eddy's, and he accepted their suggestion that he publish *Christian Science* 'silently' and donate 'King Leopold's Soliloquy' as a pamphlet to the Boston Congo Reform Association. As Leopold said in that soliloquy, 'Business is business.'

Opposite *Madison Square Garden by W. Louis Sonntag, about 1895*

Left *With Maxim Gorky at Young Writers' Club, New York, April 1906. 'I am a revolutionist,' but a prudent one.* Centre *Battle of Quinga, Philippines, 1899. Lithograph by Kurz and Allison. 'Christendom, returning bedraggled, besmirched and dishonored from pirate raids.'* Right *Last visit to Hannibal, May 1902. 'A delectable land.'*

speakers stoned from the platform, and free speech strangled by hordes of furious men who in their secret hearts are still at one with those stoned speakers—as earlier—but do not dare to say so. And now the whole nation—pulpit and all—will take up the war-cry, and shout itself hoarse, and mob any honest man who ventures to open his mouth; and presently such mouths will cease to open. Next the statesmen will invent cheap lies, putting the blame upon the nation that is attacked, and every man will be glad of those conscience-soothing falsities, and will diligently study them and refuse to examine any refutations of them; and thus he will by and by convince himself that the war is just, and will thank God for the better sleep he enjoys after this process of grotesque self-deception.

One dark parenthesis interrupted the triumphs of Mark Twain's last decade. In 1902 Livy lapsed into her last, long illness, and during the next two years there were periods when he was allowed only brief visits with her; on their thirty-third wedding anniversary, in February 1903, he saw her for five minutes. It was one of the crushing ironies of their marriage that after all these years he had been singled out by Livy's doctors, and implicitly by Livy herself, as a chief factor in the acute nervous states of exhaustion and distress that went along with hyperthyroid heart disease. On the advice of doctors they moved to Italy toward the end of 1903, but in Florence she grew steadily weaker, and although she talked about changing villas that summer it was clear that she had given up. After a brief remission, when she suddenly looked bright and young again, Clemens detected in her gaze 'that pathetic something which betrays the secret of a waning hope'.

When she died on 5 June 1904, at the age of fifty-nine, the event affected him not like the thunderclap of Susy's death but as something long expected. Looking at her for the last time, he remembered the face he had first seen in her brother's ivory miniature, and he was 'full of remorse for things done and said in the thirty-four years of married life that hurt Livy's heart'. A few weeks later he made note of 'a calamity. . . . I cannot reproduce Livy's face in my mind.' He described himself, in characteristic terms, as feeling penniless, fifty million dollars in debt.

For years, with threats of litigation and hellfire, Mark Twain had repulsed outsiders who threatened to invade his privacy and his past by publishing private letters or writing biographies. If his story was going to be told, it was going to be told his way and no other. He would have agreed with Henry Adams, who in his *Education* fabled his autobiography as a 'shield of protection in the grave' and then advised Henry James to 'take your own life in the same way, in order to prevent biographers from taking it in theirs'. With this end in mind, Clemens had been writing or dictating autobiography off and on since the 1870s, when he wrote some fragments about the Tennessee land and his early years in Florida, Missouri. Nevertheless, in January 1906, aware that he was something of a historical fixture with obligations to history, Clemens appointed as his authorized biographer (and eventual literary executor) Albert Bigelow Paine, a forty-four-year-old writer of fiction for children, author of a distinguished biography of Thomas Nast, and lifelong admirer of both Mark Twain and Joan of Arc. Paine was granted access—severely controlled access, he soon realized—to Mark Twain's privacies, papers, and friends.

At first, as source material for the biography, Clemens, lying in bed at 21 Fifth Avenue, dictated long answers to Paine's questions. These answers soon turned into daily monologues which were taken down by a stenographer and now make up the greater part of Mark Twain's published and unpublished autobiography. Biographies, he declared, 'are but the clothes and buttons of the man—the biography of the man himself cannot be written':

His acts and his words are merely the visible, thin crust of his world, with its scattered snow summits and its vacant wastes of water—and they are so trifling a part of his bulk! a mere skin enveloping it. The mass of him is

hidden—it and its volcanic fires that toss and boil, and never rest, night nor day.

He wanted his own story, his autobiography, to reveal the volcanic boil as well as the snow summits and thereby to become the truest book in the world. In one of his *Pudd'nhead Wilson* maxims he had said, 'Truth is the most valuable thing we have. Let us economize it.' Now, in his dictations, he planned to be a spendthrift, and he was delighted when Howells, after reading an installment, told him, 'You are nakeder than Adam and Eve put together, and truer than sin.' For two and a half years Mark Twain spun out his wild and wonderful history in something like half a million words of typescript, and he lived in a creative ecstasy of talking, talking, talking. Each morning he took up whatever subject interested him at the moment, and he developed it whatever its logical or chronological direction might be. His method was associative, naturalistic, random, utterly and joyously free—he delighted in its 'dewy and breezy and woodsy freshness'. In a week's work, humor, satire, nostalgia, and autobiography proper would be all mixed together, and to the same extent that autobiography had always entered Mark Twain's fiction, fiction inevitably entered his autobiography, sometimes in unintended but wholly emblematic ways.

There is, for example, a manuscript titled 'Macfarlane', which Paine printed in his edition of the autobiography and which he and some subsequent biographers used as documentation for the winter of 1856-7, when Clemens was working as a printer in Cincinnati. There he is supposed to have met and been deeply influenced by 'Macfarlane', a self-taught philosopher, whose thought paralleled Darwin's but who had concluded that with man the evolutionary scheme had finally collapsed and gone to 'wreck and ruin'. But it is now evident that Macfarlane was as much a fictional character as the Mysterious Stranger and that the manuscript, despite its characteristic autobiographical framework, was not autobiography at all but part of a philosophic and polemic tale of the sort Mark Twain was writing during the dark and despairing 1890s.

Only a few weeks after they began work together, Paine realized that many of Clemens's spellbinding reminiscences 'bore only an atmospheric relation to history'. He could recount, with absolute conviction, something that had happened only the day before, but he turned the essential circumstances around, and when Paine ventured to correct him he seemed to be startled, as if he had just waked up. 'When I was

Opposite *At seventy*

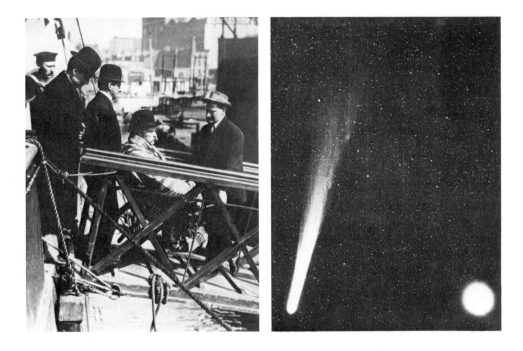

Left *His last photograph: returning to New York from Bermuda, 14 April 1910.*
Right *'It will be the greatest disappointment of my life if I don't go out with
Halley's comet.'*

younger I could remember anything, whether it happened or not,' he
said to Paine, 'but I am getting old, and soon I shall remember only the
latter.' And there are, in fact, and with only occasional cautions from
Mark Twain, parts of his autobiography to which the question of
'whether it happened' is not much more pertinent than it is to Simon
Wheeler's account of the celebrated jumping frog of Calaveras County.

But Mark Twain 'told the truth, mainly', as Huck said, various kinds
of truth. The truth to himself, for one. Freely, jubilantly, with a savage
delight, he poured out the deflected angers and opinions of a lifetime,
settled old scores with man and God. Nearly forty years after Mrs
Thomas Bailey Aldrich snubbed him in Boston, having assumed he was
drunk because of the eccentric costume he wore and his attenuated
drawl, he brought her to life in the pages of his autobiography 'un-
damaged, and just the same old thing she had always been, undeodorized
and not a whiff of her missing'. 'I conceived an aversion for her the first
time I ever saw her,' he said, 'a strange and vanity-devoured, destestable
woman! I do not believe I could ever learn to like her except on a raft at

sea with no other provisions in sight.' At the other end of the chain of being, Mark Twain dictated passages about God, passages which, he said, would probably get his heirs and assigns burned at the stake if they dared take them out of his box of posthumous stuff and publish them before A.D. 2006. (Today these dictations seem relatively harmless.)

Mark Twain's autobiography contains some of the truth *about* himself as well, even though, he reasoned, this truth might have to be deduced from his own inevitable lies, evasions, self-justifications, and reticences. 'The remorseless truth *is* there, between the lines, where the author-cat is raking dust upon it which hides from the disinterested spectator neither it nor its smell.' Finally, there is the truth of Mark Twain's own, authentic voice as he summed up three-quarters of a century of his own history and his country's. For the unifying principle of this rich and sprawling narrative is the rhythm and accent and attack of Mark Twain's voice, preserved in a written prose from which he was careful not to eliminate those conversational slips, halts, stumbles, and afterthoughts which added up to 'the subtle something which makes good talk so much better than the best imitation of it that can be done with a pen'. The like of his talk, Howells said, we shall never know again, and as a record of magnificent talk, magical, passionate, hilarious, savage, and tender, the autobiography is one of Mark Twain's masterpieces, and his last.

When his daughter Jean died of an epileptic seizure around Christmas 1909, an old man who suffered from coronary disease and was lonely in his hilltop villa in Connecticut set down his account of her life and sudden end. It was only then, with Halley's comet swimming into view again in the night skies, that he considered both his autobiography and his life to be finished. 'It is the final chapter,' he told Paine, 'I shall never write any more.' Four months later, on 21 April 1910, Mark Twain was dead.

Chapter Nine

'Speaking from the grave'

'Be good and you will be lonesome', Mark Twain said. More to the point, in April 1910, was another maxim of his. 'Let us endeavor so to live that when we come to die even the undertaker will be sorry.' Thousands of mourners came to the Brick Presbyterian Church on Fifth Avenue to file past the casket, topped with a single wreath of Stormfield laurel, where he lay in a white suit. After burial in Elmira, Mark Twain began the posthumous life which, over the next half century and more, grew more vigorous the longer he was dead, but only after a certain decline and a few grotesque adventures.

In 1916, for example, Albert Bigelow Paine presented, first as a magazine serial in *Harper's* and then as a book, Mark Twain's *The Mysterious Stranger, A Romance*. Paine had access to a number of different versions of the story composed between 1897 and 1905 and put aside, the author being satisfied with none of them. One version was set in 'St. Petersburg' (Hannibal) in the 1840s; a second in Eseldorf, Austria, in 1702; a third in Hannibal again; and a fourth in a print shop in Austria in 1490. According to John S. Tuckey and William M. Gibson, two scholars who in 1963 and 1969, respectively, published their studies of the original manuscripts, Paine performed a remarkable editorial operation, with the encouragement of Harper and Brothers. Without comment or explanation to the reader, Paine settled upon the second of Mark Twain's versions and cut it substantially. Beyond supplying new transitions, name changes, and a number of other important (but consistently silent) revisions and bowdlerizings, including the substitution of an astrologer for a bad priest as villain of the story, he managed to graft on,

Opposite *After funeral services at the Brick Presbyterian Church, New York*

at the end, a heavily edited version of a chapter from version four. The effect of this last chapter, in which Satan dismisses all reality as a 'foolish dream', is to contort the preceding narrative, to convince the reader that Mark Twain himself had finished *The Mysterious Stranger* and had been satisfied with it, and also to trap Mark Twain into the role of a sort of cosmic philosopher of solipsism.

According to Professor Gibson, Paine 'altered the manuscript of the book in a fashion that almost certainly would have enraged the author, 'secretly tried to fill Mark Twain's shoes', and 'tampered with the faith of Mark Twain's readers'. *The Mysterious Stranger* in its official version is 'an editorial fraud', says Gibson, who, in recognition of certain recurrent themes and episodes in Mark Twain's life, could also have termed it a 'hoax'. After this episode it was only fitting that in 1917 Mark Twain's posthumous vitality should have manifested itself in a published novel, *Jap Herron*, which Mrs Emily Grant Hutchings, of Hannibal, its author or amanuensis, alleged the spirit of Mark Twain had dictated to her by means of her Ouija board. At this point Harper and Brothers applied for a restraining injunction against Mrs Hutchings's publisher and argued that Mark Twain, in spirit as well as legally construable intention, was under exclusive contract to them.

At the end of 1910 William Dean Howells published *My Mark Twain*, a loving, intimate, and life-giving portrait of 'the Lincoln of our literature'. Edmund Wilson has called it 'probably the best "character" of Mark Twain we have'. Two years later Paine published his monumental biography in three volumes. It is as indispensable an account as Mark Twain's autobiography, about half of which Paine edited for publication in 1924, and in almost all respects Paine's biography is a more reliable and comprehensive source, especially for the later years. Paine dug into the box of posthumous stuff for *The Mysterious Stranger*; *Mark Twain's Letters* (1917); *Europe and Elsewhere* (1923), which included several suppressed writings—'The United States of Lyncherdom', 'The War Prayer', and 'Corn-Pone Opinions'; and in 1935, two years before Paine died, *Mark Twain's Notebook*, a tantalizingly brief volume of selections from the thirty-eight notebooks which, along with a vast treasure of letters, manuscripts, and documents, are now in the Mark Twain Papers at the University of California, Berkeley. In the course of his long tenure as literary editor Paine consistently rejected applications for access to these papers; he argued, according to his successor, Bernard DeVoto, that there was nothing new to be learned or said about Mark Twain. Paine recalled his own difficulties in establishing a proprietary claim to Mark Twain's 'truth'. But he also had to face the fact that in old age, a familiar time of escalating narcissism coupled with physical and psychic degeneration, Mark Twain had been more vivid than lovable in many personal aspects. It was protection Paine had in mind when he confided to Harper and Brothers in 1926:

> I think on general principles it is a mistake to let any one else write about Mark Twain, as long as we can prevent it. . . . As soon as this is begun (writing about him at all, I mean) the Mark Twain that we have 'preserved'— the Mark Twain that we knew, the traditional Mark Twain—will begin to fade and change, and with that process the Harper Mark Twain property will depreciate.

During the twenty-five years immediately after Mark Twain's death something sad, ironic, and closely connected with the dynamics of celebrity, happened to his reputation. He complained that he had to suppress his true opinions, and he even regarded himself as something of a heresiarch, but none the less he became a beloved family author. His readers valued him chiefly as a writer of boys' books (and in particular *Tom Sawyer* rather than *Huckleberry Finn*); as a genial humorist whose dark comments on man and society (with the exception of *The Mysterious Stranger*) could be considered tiltings merely aberrant and testy; as the hero of a thousand funny anecdotes, many of them apocryphal; and as

Left *Albert Bigelow Paine.* Right *Clara Clemens*

mirror and laughing philosopher for the era of normality that America
is supposed to have entered at the end of the First World War. Among
the fixtures of civilization in Sinclair Lewis's Gopher Prairie are silos,
phonographs, leather-upholstered Morris chairs, oil stocks, and unread
sets of Mark Twain. The fate of many another standard author overtook
Mark Twain; his work began to fulfill his own definition of a classic as
'a book which people praise and don't read'.

In 1920, the year Lewis published *Main Street* (its feeling for colloquial
speech and rhythms owed a great deal to Mark Twain), Van Wyck
Brooks questioned the man, his achievement, and the times and backgrounds that fostered (or smothered) him in *The Ordeal of Mark Twain*.
According to Brooks, Mark Twain was a tragic failure as writer and
artist. He was 'a victim of arrested development' and a 'spiritual
valetudinarian', having been emasculated into timidity, compromise,
and mere entertainment by his mother and Livy and by forces of gentility,
commerce, and tradition which could be observed in the frontier setting
of Hannibal as well as in Elmira and Hartford. Brooks sometimes
reasoned from frail data to sweeping conclusions, but even those conclusions demanded answers; for he wrote what remains the most brilliant, challenging, and provocative of all studies of Mark Twain. Not
the least of his many services was that by probing Mark Twain's inner
and outer conflictiveness, Brooks rescued him from deadly stereotypes:
the genial humorist and entertainer; the cosmic philosopher; and the
single-minded critic of capitalist society, a people's critical realist, which
is the role he has been given in the Soviet Union, where he is as popular
as Jack London and O. Henry.

Brooks's view of Mark Twain as a failure was challenged by Bernard
DeVoto, who argued that frontier America was richer and more nurtur-
ing for a writer than anyone had realized. *Mark Twain's America*
(1932)—pointedly described by DeVoto as 'an essay in the correction of
ideas'—may, in rebuttal of Brooks, have made too much of a case for the
West and too little for what Mark Twain derived from the East. By
1942, when he published *Mark Twain at Work*, DeVoto had succeeded
Paine as editor of the Mark Twain Papers, had studied the unpublished
material relating to Mark Twain's ordeal of the late 1890s, and had also
gone through some dialectical process by which he arrived at a position
remarkably sympathetic to Brooks's. And by this time Brooks had
written his several celebrations of nineteenth-century American literature and culture and was less disposed to deal with Mark Twain as a
cautionary life bearing out the claim Brooks had made in 1921, that
'for half a century the American writer as a type has gone down to
defeat'.

Partly through the Brooks-DeVoto debate, partly through the opening of the Mark Twain Papers to scholars and writers, partly through a more subtle and complex view of the American past as a whole, Mark Twain has been liberated to be something like himself—a deeply conflicted and totally unique figure, brilliantly but intermittently fulfilled. More and more his lifework and lifestyle are read not in terms of simplisms and stereotypes but as the hard-won resolution of the many disunities and identities of Samuel Clemens and Mark Twain.

An enormous scholarly, critical, and biographical literature has sprung up, especially since the end of the Second World War. *Huckleberry Finn*, once scorned by official culture and banned from certain schools and libraries, has now been so studied, annotated, and quarreled over that it has become a sort of fresh-water *Moby Dick*, and it is possible, in the extravagance of this re-recognition of Mark Twain, that some of his darker books, *Pudd'nhead Wilson*, for example, have been overvalued at the expense of happier works such as *Roughing It*. Cycles of correspondence that Paine did not see (Mark Twain's letters to Mary Mason Fairbanks) or was not permitted to see in full (the letters to Livy and to Howells) have now been published with such a richness and scrupulosity of supporting information that the editions are biographies in themselves. *Letters from the Earth*, a brilliant collection of heterodoxies, was edited for publication by Bernard DeVoto in 1939, but it was not until 1960, half a century after Mark Twain's death and four years after DeVoto's, that the surviving daughter, Clara Clemens Samossoud, gave permission for it to be published.

Paine's fears to the contrary, the reputation and popularity of Mark Twain have never stood higher than they do now. At no time since his death have his work and spirit seemed quite so apt, so welcome, so contemporary. His strategy of 'speaking from the grave' displayed, with good reason, 'the calm confidence of a Christian with four aces'.

Illustration Acknowledgments

Abbreviations
MTHB   Mark Twain Home Board, Hannibal.
Photos: Don Sigler
MTP   Mark Twain Papers, University of
California, Berkeley
MTM   Mark Twain Memorial, Hartford
LOC   Library of Congress
NYPL   New York Public Library
MCNY   Museum of the City of New York
Page 10 From *Das Weltgebände* by Dr M.
Wilhelm Meyer, 1898
Page 13 MTHB
Page 14 Radio Times Hulton Picture Library
Page 17 The St Louis Art Museum
Page 18 *Above* Collection of Edgar William
and Bernice Chrysler Garbisch. *Below* Mis-
souri Historical Society
Page 21 MTP
Page 22 *Left* LOC. *Right* MTHB
Page 23 MTHB
Pages 26–7 The St Louis Art Museum
Page 29 Portrait of Mark Twain: MTP.
Washington: Mary Evans Picture Library
Page 30 *Left* Brown Brothers. *Right* From
*Aalteekeningen op eene reis door de Vereenigde
Staten Van Nord Amerika in 1859*
Page 31 Chicago Historical Society
Page 32 From *Life on the Mississippi*, 1883
Page 33 MTHB
Page 35 MCNY
Page 36 *Both* LOC
Page 38 LOC
Page 40 Courtesy of the Suffolk Museum and
Carriage House at Story Brook, N.Y
Page 42 Kennedy Galleries
Page 43 Thomas Gilcrease Institute of Ameri-
can History and Art, Tulsa, Oklahoma

Page 45 *Above* Los Angeles Athletic Club.
Below Stanford University Museum of Art.
Gift of Mrs Jane L. Stanford
Pages 46–7 Nelson Gallery, Atkins Museum
Page 48 LOC
Pages 50–1 NYPL
Page 52 *Left* From *Roughing It*, 1875. *Right*
Bancroft Library, Berkeley
Page 53 *Left* Bancroft Library, Berkeley.
Right Nevada State Historical Society
Page 55 LOC
Page 56 *Left* From *The Savage Club* by Aaron
Watson, 1907. Courtesy of The Savage Club.
Centre MacKay School of Mines, University
of Nevada, Reno. *Right* LOC
Page 57 Bancroft Library, Berkeley
Page 61 Mary Evans Picture Library
Page 63 *Left* LOC. *Right* From *Hawaii, the
Past, Present and Future of its Island King-
dom*, by Manley Hopkins, 1862
Page 65 From *The Annals of San Francisco*,
1855. California Historical Society
Page 66 From *Harper's Bazaar*, 1873.
Courtesy of the New York Historical Society,
New York City
Pages 70–1 The Metropolitan Museum of Art
Page 73 MCNY
Page 74 National Museum of Wales
Page 76 MTP
Page 77 From *La Comédie de Notre Temps,
Petite Nana*. Bibliothèque Nationale.
Giraudon
Page 78 From *The Innocents Abroad*, 1875
Page 80 *Left* MCNY. *Above right* MTP. *Below
right* Dickens Rare Print Collection, London
University
Page 82 Brown Brothers

Illustration Acknowledgments

Page 85 *Above* and *Below centre* Buffalo and Erie Historical Society. *Below left* Justin Kaplan. *Below right* MTM
Page 88 From *Philadelphia 1609–1884*, by J. Thomas Scharf, 1884
Page 91 MCNY
Page 92 LOC
Pages 94–5 Mansell Collection
Page 96 Mark Twain, Library and Quarry Farm: MTM. Prospect Street and Warner House: Connecticut Historical Society
Page 99 Mary Evans Picture Library
Page 101 From *Vanity Fair*, 1879. Photo: Derrick Witty
Pages 102–3 MTM. Photo: Meyer Studios
Page 104 MTM. Photo: Meyer Studios
Page 106 *All* MTM
Page 107 LOC
Page 108 From *The Adventures of Tom Sawyer*, 1876
Page 111 *Left* Courtesy of The New York Historical Society, New York City. *Right* LOC
Page 113 A. F. Kersting
Page 114 LOC
Page 116 *Both* LOC
Page 119 *Left* Mansell Collection. *Right* Bayreuther Festspiele
Page 120 Harlingue-Viollet
Page 122 MTM
Page 124 Connecticut Historical Society
Page 125 Courtesy of USMA Archives
Page 126 *Both* Missouri Historical Society
Page 129 Courtesy of The New York Historical Society, New York City
Page 131 LOC
Page 132 The Corcoran Gallery of Art
Page 134 MTM
Page 135 J. Clarence Davies Collection, MCNY
Page 136 *Above* From *The Adventures of Huckleberry Finn*, 1884. *Below* MTHB
Page 138 MTP
Page 140 LOC
Page 142 MTP
Page 143 *Left* From *A Connecticut Yankee*. *Centre* Tate Gallery. *Right* Mary Evans Picture Library
Page 145 Chicago Historical Society
Page 147 From *Harper's Weekly*, 1886. Chicago Historical Society
Page 149 From *The Eglinton Tournament*, 1843. Courtesy of Ian Anstruther

Page 150 Bibliothèque Nationale
Page 153 LOC
Page 154 *Left* H. Roger Viollet. *Right* Bryn Mawr College Library
Page 156 *Above left* Brown Brothers. *Above centre* Exxon. *Above right* George Rainbird Ltd. *Below* LOC
Page 158 MTHB
Page 159 *Left* Mansell Collection. *Right* Mary Evans Picture Library
Page 161 MTM
Page 162 Guildford Reference Library
Page 164 Mansell Collection
Page 167 The Lotos Club
Page 168 Courtesy of Walter Grill. Photo: Ludwig Steichele
Page 170 *Left* Mansell Collection. *Right* From *Smithsonian Report*, 1916. LOC
Page 173 Yale University Library
Page 174 From *Vanity Fair*, 1899. Mansell Collection
Page 175 Nevada State Historical Society
Page 177 Piccadilly Gallery
Pages 178–9 Albertina, Vienna
Page 180 Tate Gallery
Page 182 MTP
Page 184 Milton Meltzer, *Mark Twain Himself*
Page 186 Byron Collection, MCNY
Page 189 *Above left* Justin Kaplan. *Above centre* MTM. *Above right* The Savage Club. Photo: Derrick Witty. *Below* Byron Collection, MCNY
Page 191 *Above left* MTP. *Above centre* Brown Brothers. *Above right* MTM. *Below* Radio Times Hulton Picture Library
Page 192 *Left* Berg Collection, NYPL. *Right* LOC
Page 195 Yale University Library
Page 197 Museum of Art, Carnegie Institute
Pages 198–9 Whitney Museum of American Art
Page 200 MCNY
Page 202 *Left* Soviet Weekly. *Centre* LOC. *Right* MTP
Page 204 Milton Meltzer, *Mark Twain Himself*
Page 206 *Left* Milton Meltzer, *Mark Twain Himself*. *Right* Science Museum, London
Page 208 MTM
Page 211 *Left* MTP. *Right* MTHB

Text Sources

Certain portions of the text have been adapted by the author from his *Mr Clemens and Mark Twain* (New York: Simon and Schuster, 1966).

In the notes, which are keyed to the text by page number and catch phrase, the following abbreviations and short titles are used:

AU-1924 Albert Bigelow Paine, ed., *Mark Twain's Autobiography*. New York: Harper, 1924.

AU-1959 Charles Neider, ed., *The Autobiography of Mark Twain*. New York: Harper, 1959.

Brown Franklin Walker and G. Ezra Dane, eds., *Mark Twain's Travels with Mr Brown*. New York: Knopf, 1940.

Eruption Bernard DeVoto, ed., *Mark Twain in Eruption*. New York: Harper, 1940.

HH&T Walter Blair, ed., *Mark Twain's Hannibal, Huck & Tom*. Berkeley and Los Angeles: University of California Press, 1969.

L Albert Bigelow Paine, ed., *Mark Twain's Letters*. 2 vols. New York: Harper, 1917.

LL Dixon Wecter, ed., *The Love Letters of Mark Twain*. New York: Harper, 1949.

MTH Henry N. Smith and William M. Gibson, eds., *Mark Twain—Howells Letters*. 2 vols. Cambridge, Mass.: Harvard University Press, 1960.

MTN Albert Bigelow Paine, ed., *Mark Twain's Notebook*. New York: Harper, 1935.

MTP Mark Twain Papers, University of California Library, Berkeley.

Paine Albert Bigelow Paine, *Mark Twain, A Biography*. 3 vols. New York: Harper, 1912.

Portable Bernard DeVoto, ed., *The Portable Mark Twain*. New York: Viking, 1946.

Rogers Lewis Leary, ed., *Mark Twain's Correspondence with Henry Huttleston Rogers, 1893–1909*. Los Angeles and Berkeley: University of California Press, 1969.

SCH Dixon Wecter. *Sam Clemens of Hannibal*. Boston: Houghton Mifflin, 1952.

SLC Samuel L. Clemens

Speeches Mark Twain's Speeches. New York: Harper, 1923.

TIA D. M. McKeithan, ed., *Traveling with the Innocents Abroad*. Norman, Okla.: University of Oklahoma Press, 1958.

W Albert Bigelow Paine, ed., *The Writings of Mark Twain*. 'Definitive Edition', 37 vols. New York: Harper, 1922–5.

Chapter One

Page 14 'She was of a sunshiny disposition': 'Jane Lampton Clemens', in *HH&T*, pp. 52, 53.

Page 14 'stern, unsmiling': 'Villagers of 1840–3', in *HH&T*, p. 39.

Page 15 'the heavy curse of prospective wealth': *AU*-1959, pp. 22, 25.

Page 15 'He did not say goodbye': 'Villagers of 1840–3', in *HH&T*, pp. 29–40. On 'The Autopsy' see also *SCH*, pp. 116–17.

Page 16 'My father died': SLC to Clara Clemens, 24 March 1910 (MTP).

Page 19 'From the cradle up': *AU*-1959, p. 43.

Page 19 'It all seems so small': Paine, p. 1168.

Page 19 'The Dandy Frightening the Squatter': reprinted in Franklin J. Meine, ed., *Tall Tales of the Southwest*. New York: Alfred A. Knopf, 1930, p. 445.

Page 20 'The first house was built': SLC's *American Courier* sketch privately issued by Roger Butterfield as a keepsake presentation to the Antiquarian Booksellers' Association of America, 1967.

Page 20 According to Dixon Wecter: *SCH*, p. 60.

Page 22 'introduced the change': 'Villagers of 1840–3', in *HH&T*, p. 35.

Page 22 'The class lines': 'Jane Lampton Clemens'. in *HH&T*, p. 46.

Text Sources

Page 23 'Opened with prayer': 'Villagers of 1840–3', in *HH&T*, p. 37.
Page 24 He witnessed other killings: *AU*-1959, pp. 40–42.
Page 24 'The part of my education': *AU*-1924, I, pp. 109–15.
Page 25 New York in the summer of 1853: *L*, pp. 21–5.
Page 28 'One isn't a printer ten years': 'The Turning-Point of My Life', *W*, XXVI, p. 136.
Page 28 'I worked, not diligently': *Eruption*, p. 303.
Page 30 'the native of the mountains': 'The Turning-Point of My Life', *W*, XXVI, pp. 132–3.
Page 30 Under Bixby, Clemens learned: *Life on the Mississippi*, Chapters 8–10.
Page 31 'I loved the profession': *Life on the Mississippi*, Chapter 14.
Page 32 'What man dare': *Is Shakespeare Dead?* New York: Harper, 1909, pp. 5–6.
Page 34 'I yelled for a rope': Paine, p. 149.
Page 34 'When I find a well-drawn character': *Life on the Mississippi*, Chapter 18.
Page 34 'emerge from boyhood': Pascal Covici, jr, ed., 'Dear Master Wattie: the Mark Twain—David Watt Bowser Letters', *Southwest Review*, XLV, No. 2 (spring 1960), pp. 107–8.
Page 34 'My nightmares': Notebook No. 16 (MTP).
Page 37 'Henry died this morning': SLC telegram to William A. Moffett. 21 June 1858 (MTP).
Page 37 'never *does* do anything': Samuel C. Webster, ed., *Mark Twain, Business Man*. Boston: Little, Brown, 1946, pp. 55–6, 53.
Page 37 'There was a good deal of confusion': 'The Private History of a Campaign That Failed', *W*, XV, p. 255.
Page 38 'I reckon I had better black my face': SLC to Jane Lampton Clemens, in Minnie M. Brashear, *Mark Twain, Son of Missouri*, Chapel Hill: University of North Carolina Press, 1934, pp. 153–5.
Page 39 'I was a *soldier* two weeks once': SLC to unidentified person, 1890, *Portable*, p. 774.

Chapter Two
Page 41 'The birds': *L*, p. 54.
Page 41 'Washoe Zephyr': *Roughing It*, Chapter 21.
Page 42 'A little bit of a man': *Roughing It*, Chapter 8.

Page 42 'We felt that there was only one': *Roughing It*, Chapter 3.
Page 42 'the "livest" town': *Roughing It*, Part II, Chapter 2.
Page 44 'Within half an hour': *Roughing It*, Chapter 23.
Page 44 'I've been a prospector': SLC to unidentified person, 1890, *Portable*, p. 779.
Page 44 'I own one eighth': *L*, pp. 73–4.
Page 44 a bundle of deeds and certificates: in MTP.
Page 49 'The fact is': *L*, p. 82.
Page 52 'dashed into Carson on horseback': 'Latest Sensation', in Virginia City *Territorial Enterprise*, 28 October 1863; reprinted in Ivan Benson, *Mark Twain's Western Years*. Stanford, Calif.: Stanford University Press, 1938, pp. 176–7.
Page 53 'It was the talk of the town': 'My Bloody Massacre', in *Mark Twain's Sketches*. Hartford: American Publishing Company, 1875, p. 245.
Page 53 'It is my unsolicited opinion': 'Letter from Mark Twain', in Virginia City *Territorial Enterprise*; reprinted in Henry Nash Smith, ed., *Mark Twain of the Enterprise*. Berkeley and Los Angeles: University of California Press, 1957, pp. 159–60.
Page 54 'I am prone to boast': *L*, 91.
Page 56 The evening ended: *L*, p. 183.
Page 56 a curious episode: the relevant documents are in *Mark Twain of the Enterprise*, pp. 190–205.
Page 59 'Coleman with his jumping frog': *MTN*, p. 7.
Page 59 'Between you and I': *LL*, p. 41.
Page 60 'I never had but two *powerful* ambitions': MTP.
Page 60 'I am generally placed': *L*, p. 102.
Page 62 'trimmed and trained and schooled me': *L*, pp. 182–3.
Page 62 'Many times I have been sorry': SLC marginal comment, 21 April 1909, in his copy of J. R. Lowell's *Letters*, as quoted in Los Angeles *Times*, 15 April 1951.
Page 64 'simple soldier, who, all untaught': *Speeches*, p. 137.

Chapter Three
Page 67 'Make your mark in New York': *Brown*, p. 176.
Page 67 'There is something about this ceaseless buzz': *Brown*, p. 260.
Page 68 'Honest poverty': *Brown*, p. 236.

217

Page 69 '*Any* lecture of mine': *LL*, pp. 165–6.
Page 69 lectured in Hannibal: *Brown*, pp. 143–6.
Page 69 'One of the greatest liars': Paine, p. 107.
Page 70 'so cheerful and handsomely built': *Brown*, pp. 156–7.
Page 71 'It is full of damnable errors': *L*, p. 124.
Page 72 'the surprising fact': *AU*-1959, pp. 272–3.
Page 72 'the *last* link': 'The Turning-Point .of My Life', *W*, XXVI, p. 136.
Page 72 'When a subscription book of mine': *Rogers*, p. 249.
Page 75 'I basked': *W*, I, p. 11.
Page 76 The citizens of Torre Annunziata: *TIA*, p. 84.
Page 77 'The ancients considered': *TIA*, p 19.
Page 78 'Harte read all the MS.': SLC to C. H. Webb, 26 November 1870 (photostat in MTP).
Page 79 'I saw her first': *AU*-1959, p. 183.
Page 80 'made the fortune of my life': *AU*-1959, p. 174.
Page 81 'heart-free laugh of a girl': *AU*-1959, p. 185.
Page 81 'I do not regret': *LL*, pp. 18–20.
Page 81 'I believe in you': *LL*, p. 25.
Page 83 'Almost the only crime': SLC to Clara Clemens. 20 May 1905 (MTP).
Page 84 'The fountains of my great deep': SLC to Will Bowen. 6 February 1870. Theodore Hornberger, ed., *Mark Twain's Letters to Will Bowen*. Austin: University of Texas Press, 1941, pp. 18–21.
Page 86 'most celebrated man in America': SLC to J. H. Riley, 3 March 1871 (MTP).
Page 87 'one might have supposed': *AU*-1959, p. 126.

Chapter Four
Page 89 'morality and huckleberries': *Alta California*, 6 September 1868.
Page 90 'I am as uplifted': *MTH*, pp. 10–11.
Page 93 'I have seen an entire family': 'Speech on Accident Insurance', in *Mark Twain's Sketches* (Hartford, 1875), pp. 229–30.
Page 98 'What is the chief end of man?': 'The Revised Catechism', New York *Tribune*, 27 September 1871.
Page 100 'This nation is not reflected': SLC to Orion Clemens, 27 March 1875 (MTP).
Page 105 'simply a hymn': *L*, p. 477.

Page 105 'boyhood & youth': quoted in Hamlin Hill, 'The Composition and Structure of *Tom Sawyer*', *American Literature*, XXXII, No. 4 (January 1961), p. 386.
Page 106 'Began another boys' book': *MTH*, p. 144.
Page 108 'Yes, one of the brightest gems': *Speeches*, p. 55.
Page 109 'I never saw a play': quoted in Joseph Daly, *The Life of Augustin Daly* (New York, 1917), pp. 235–6.
Page 110 'If you fight as well as you feed': SLC's speech is in *The 240th Annual Record of the Ancient and Honorable Artillery Company of Massachusetts* (Boston, 1878), pp. 3–30.
Page 110 'The man was not in uniform': *W*, XV, pp. 278–9.
Page 111 Whittier birthday dinner: *Speeches*, pp. 63–76.
Page 112 'I do not ask you to forgive': 27 December 1877 (MTP).
Page 117 'I know you will refrain': *MTN*, p. 131.
Page 117 Germany was a paradise: *MTH*, p. 227.
Page 117 'Geborn 1835': SLC to Bayard Taylor, 7 May 1878. *American Literature*, VIII, No. 1 (March 1936), p. 48.
Page 117 'hot biscuits, *real* coffee': *MTN*, p. 149.
Page 117 'a great chorus': *A Tramp Abroad*, Chapter 9.
Page 118 'I don't ever seem to be': *MTH*, pp. 248–9.
Page 118 'To send this nasty creature': *MTH*, p. 235.
Page 118 'The motion of a raft': *A Tramp Abroad*, Chapter 14.
Page 120 'My sluggish soul': *MTH*, p. 274.
Page 121 'The babies': *Speeches*, pp. 58–62.

Chapter Five
Page 126 'such booming working-days': *L*, p. 434.
Page 127 'the bane of Americans': 12 May 1880 (MTP).
Page 130 'a book of mine': Notebook No. 28A (MTP).
Page 137 'Huck, that abused child of mine': Julia Chandler Harris, *The Life and Letters of Joel Chandler Harris* (Boston, 1918), p. 566.
Page 137 His swan song: *MTH*, pp. 610–11.
Page 138 'Indeed I have been misjudged': *L*, pp. 527–8.

Text Sources

Page 138 'Dear Sirs': MTP.
Page 139 'Dear Charley': *L*, pp. 452–3.
Page 139 'For instance, it will deter': *MTH*, pp. 877–8.

Chapter Six
Page 143 'Dream of being a knight errant': *MTN*, p. 171.
Page 143 'Have a battle': Notebook No. 18 (MTP).
Page 145 'Poor old Ma': SLC note on envelope of letter from Jane Lampton Clemens (MTP).
Page 145 'He mourns his lost land': Notebook No. 20 (MTP).
Page 148 'The change is in *me*': *MTH*, p. 595.
Page 151 'I watched over one dear project': SLC to unidentified person, 1890, *Portable*, p. 775.
Page 151 'If it were only to write over again': *MTH*, p. 613.
Page 154 'Travel has no longer': *MTH*, p. 645.
Page 157 'You and I are a team': *Rogers*, p. 292.
Page 157 like a thunderclap: *Rogers*, pp. 108–9.
Page 158 'There's one thing': *Rogers*, p. 115.
Page 160 'I shall arrive next January': *L*, p. 629.
Page 160 'one of the mysteries of our nature': *AU*-1924, II, p. 34.
Page 160 'I have *hated* life before': *LL*, p. 324.
Page 160 'Mr. Clemens, Mr. Zola, Mr. Harte': Susy Clemens's deathbed writings are in MTP.
Page 160 'He was all dog': SLC to Pamela A. Moffett. 7 January 1897 (MTP).
Page 161 'A man's house burns down': *AU*-1924, II, p. 34.
Page 163 'I am a mud image': *MTH*, p. 664.

Chapter Seven
Page 169 'I was suddenly': *MTN*, pp. 351–2.
Page 171 Paine, p. 964.
Page 171 'we are all mad': *MTN*, p. 345.
Page 176 'He was good': *Palimpsest* (State Historical Society of Iowa), X, No. 10 (October 1929), p. 396.
Page 176 'The debts . . .': *L*, p. 653.
Page 183 'The 20th Century': *MTN*, p. 372.

Chapter Eight
Page 190 'Like all the other nations': *Eruption*, p. 65.

Page 192 'When we contemplate her': SLC to Mr Day. 21 March 1901 (MTP).
Page 192 'I am selling my Lourdes stock': Paine, p. 1076.
Page 192 'The political and commercial morals': *Eruption*, p. 81.
Page 193 'I am thankful': SLC to Editor, New York *World*, November 1907 (MTP).
Page 193 'a talk with Carnegie': *Eruption*, pp. 49–50.
Page 193 'He has bought fame': *Eruption*, p. 39.
Page 193 Judge Kenesaw Mountain Landis: Notebook No. 38 (MTP).
Page 201 'I bring you the stately matron': New York *Herald*, 30 December 1900.
Page 205 'the clothes and buttons of the man': *AU*-1924, I, p. 2.
Page 205 a manuscript titled 'Macfarlane': see Paul Baender, 'Alias Macfarlane: A Revision of Mark Twain Biography', *American Literature*, vol. XXXVIII, No. 2 (May 1966), pp. 187–97.
Page 206 Mrs Thomas Bailey Aldrich: *AU*-1959, pp. 357–64.
Page 207 'The remorseless truth': *MTH*, p. 782.
Page 207 'the subtle something': *MTH*, p. 778.

Chapter Nine
Page 209 The textual history of *The Mysterious Stranger*: John S. Tuckey, *Mark Twain and Little Satan*. West Lafayette, Indiana: Purdue University Studies, 1963. William M. Gibson, ed., *Mark Twain's Mysterious Stranger Manuscripts*. Berkeley and Los Angeles: University of California Press, 1969.
Page 210 Paine 'altered the manuscript . . .': Gibson, pp. 1–3.
Page 210 *Jap Herron*: Paul Fatout, 'Mark Twain: A Footnote'. *Columbia University Forum*, Fall 1960, pp. 51–2.
Page 210 Edmund Wilson: *The Shock of Recognition*. Garden City: Doubleday, and Co., 1947, p. 673.
Page 210 According to Bernard DeVoto: *Mark Twain's America*. Boston: Houghton Mifflin, Company, 1932, p. x.
Page 211 'I think on general principles': quoted in Hamlin Hill, *Mark Twain: God's Fool*. New York: Harper and Row, 1973, p. 268.

Index

Index